The Venice Book

A Personal Guide to the
City's Art & Culture

The
Venice Book

Sophie Ullin

Introduction

My baptism into the church of fine art transpired when my cosmopolitan German grandmother, Elinor, whisked me away on a six-week Grand Tour of the continent, as her mother had done before her, to inculcate me with a love of art.

One by one Lorli, as she was better known, introduced me to her cavalcade of great passions and they were many; the stained glass windows of Chartres Cathederal, the Uffizi's Gothic and Renaissance masters Simone Martine, Giotto and Piero della Francesca whom she held dear to her heart; the Gregorian chants of the monks echoing inside the magnificent Romanesque interior of San Miniato al Monte, Leonardo da Vinci's *The Last Supper* in Milan, afternoon tea alongside Gauguin and van Gogh in the home of Zurich art collectors replete with maids, the Baroque Bavarian palace of Nymphenburg and finally a visit to Frankfurt's Historisches Museum to show me the works from the collections of my great grandparents, Albert and Hedwig Ullmann. On occasion, I strayed from her cultural road map invoking sacrilege – such as the time I preferred to ride the cool, glass-encased escalators of the Centre Pompidou rather than viewing the magnificent Bonnard exhibition inside. Ultimately, in spite of the odd diversion, Lorli's cunning plan worked.

Although my grandmother and I never had the opportunity to see Venice together, she armed me with the capacity to look, to perceive, to appraise, to be enlightened. Indeed, my first encounter of *La Serenissima* was on a misty winter's day just after Christmas in the late 1980s with a Milanese family friend. It was a tantalising taste and I vowed to return. Some five years later I found myself at the opening week of the Art Biennale known as the Vernissage with my father, Claude, where we delighted in the energy and magnetism that characterises the wonderland world of Venice at full art throttle. Ever since, in my role as an art advisor, my Venetian adventures have been inextricably intertwined with the Biennale and from the early 2000s I have been joined in the 'pilgrimage' by my equally passionate contemporary art clients. On each occasion the city imparts another perspective, another hue, spoiling me with a rich retinue of memories and experiences upon which to add to my Venetian arsenal of wonder.

Outside of my own experience, romantic notions of Venice universally endure: mix an ampoule of beauty with a carafe of culture and flagon of history, then add a dash of mystery, a touch of enigma, a dram of melancholy and a spoonful of secrets and you have a ravishing aphrodisiac otherwise known as Venezia. Its lustre and allure is legendary, immediately manifest in the architecture and its waterways.

Arguably Venice trades on its timelessness and is consequently perceived by visitors purely as a sublime living museum. However, this noble and grand mercantile city has always possessed a subtle elasticity, continually adapting to changing circumstances, weaving and melding tradition and reinvention proudly together. In the 21st century, Venice has faced not only the challenges of rising waters, but relentless waves of tourists who have come to view the city as a kind of Disneyworld pitstop where landmarks are clicked through and consumed with a smartphone shot to capture this approximated experience. This book offers a counterpoint, and perhaps salvation, to those who seek to move beyond this reductive, virtual prism to immerse themselves into a beguiling parallel sphere.

To this end, I have tapped on the shoulders of my confrères, who like me, are endlessly drawn to peeling back the layers from Venice's handsome facade to uncover glimmers of its enticing and bewitching underbelly. We all hold dear the belief that a love of Venice is something best shared with a mindful approach that will hopefully lead to its preservation rather than diminution. My generous and insightful band of artists, actors, designers, fashionistas, philanthropists, art advisors, curators, museum and gallery directors have opened their precious black books and memory banks to impart their nuanced perspectives as well as divulge their secret spots, hidey holes, favourite art experiences, must-go restaurants, best bars, shopping hot spots and hotel heavens.

Incontestably, this most humanist of cities cannot be reduced to a mere simulacra for *La Serenissima* thankfully possesses a power and potency that goes beyond the state of her immense physical beauty. The city also exists in the cerebral and sensual plane and with the recent influx of contemporary cultural institutions its relevance has been refreshingly reframed and context renewed whilst leaving its enigmatic nature undisrupted.

Rally

Venice Seen and Unseen

A city that was established close
to 1,600 years ago warrants many
dedicated words. However, while
not wishing to diminish its significant
history, it is described here in fairly
broad strokes presenting aspects of
Venice's story through the prism
of art and culture.

Contemporary via Renaissance

In the realm of art, Venice was a leading Renaissance light, its artists renowned for melding the pervasive Byzantine influences of gold mosaic and the innovations of oil painting from northern Europe to form their own distinct style infused with rich spirit and feeling. Artists like Giovanni Bellini promulgated the portrayal of natural light and scenes that moved beyond religious narratives to embrace the natural world; his works were saturated in brilliant, luminous colour, a feature no doubt enhanced by Venice's privileged access to the finest array of pigments as a result of its extensive trade network. The dominance and profound influence of the Venetian School continued under the command of High Renaissance artists Giorgione and Titian, who both masterfully injected a compelling combination of poetry, emotion and sense of enigma into the religious, mythological, landscape and portrait genres.

As Venice transitioned from a mercantile power to a tourist economy buoyed by devotees of The Grand Tour, the succeeding generation of artists shifted their focus towards views of the city, be they real or imagined. In panorama and highly detailed, the scenes were wrought by Canaletto and his nephew Bernardo Bellotto. Sadly, as the 18th century came to a close, the light of creativity dimmed and the city that had once been an artistic epicentre, became a repository of relics.

Venice may no longer be an atelier for prevailing art movements but it is still a centre for intriguing encounters and a sustained cultural dialogue. The crosswinds of change have been swirling in recent years and a silver thread has emerged, woven by a handful of luxury goods and textile titans under the spell of the city's enigmatic pull. Peggy Guggenheim sparked the welcome trend of private museums presenting thought-provoking contemporary art in 1951. However, 50 years later it has been collector and business magnate François Pinault along with fashion designer and philanthropist Miuccia Prada who have staged astounding and sometimes polarising exhibitions of art. Framed against the assured background of archaic tradition and classical surrounds, they have really pushed the button on relevance and reinvention. Today the promise of renewed cultural capital fuelled by the charge of contemporary art blankets the air.

Ceaseless transition is forever at the heart of
Venice (history does not have a binding lease)
and the passages between *calli* and canals, the
way Venetians transit between their islands
and to the mainland, the lapping of the waves
against the buildings and the coursing water
underneath are physical reminders of the
tradition of adaptation.

Seen and Unseen

Long before the bright lights of New York, the metropolis of Venice compelled us to swivel our gaze up, down, left, right...not merely straight ahead, to find ourselves absorbed and stimulated by the grandest as well as the most modest of details. Venice's enduring ability to reboot our powers of observation offers even greater potency today. The sensual and visceral nature of this city is fundamental to her complex core and lies at the heart of the power and the ardour she invokes.

The history of Venice's power and economy is writ large in the sophisticated articulation of its buildings and layout of its urban framework, perpetually described as labyrinthine. For centuries the citizens have adroitly played the cards of both grandeur and intimacy, the burghers and merchants strategically embellishing the Grand Canal with magnificent palazzo facades, aware of the commanding attention and political charge. They have, however, been unwilling to submit to complete exposure of their lives, closely guarding their intimate family spaces through secret gardens and obscure street entrances.

Venice endlessly seduces with its mesmeric dance between the seen and the unseen, manifest not only physically but embedded culturally into the psyche of its citizens. Perhaps no symbol better encapsulates this than the mask. In our modern minds it is wedded to the Carnevale, but the tradition of mask wearing in Venetian society has existed since the 13th century, utilised in the political arena for anonymous voting, for concealing identities without fear or favour and for the pursuit of illicit, criminal and romantic encounters alike. The respected Mascherari Guild created almost a dozen styles that could be worn for up to six months a year by its citizens who, while camouflaged and adhering to the government's rules for mask wearing could not be arrested. Quite the symbol of freedom.

During the 17th century when Venice became a favoured destination for The Grand Tour, with beauty as her calling card and Vivaldi's baroque string harmonies ringing out, the mask was pivotal in propelling her reputation as a pleasure capital in the aftermath of the Empire's fall. Refined cultural pursuits were often quickly overtaken by hedonistic adventures at the casino, where masks were de rigueur, or in hooded gondolas designed to veil the clandestine rendezvous of courtesans and their consorts. The ancient pre-Lent celebration, Carnevale, originally encouraged mask wearing as a way of dispensing with the signs of social status and gender, a cogent symbol of equality. By the late 1600s the Carnevale had metamorphosed from a religious event of sanctioned indulgence into a thrilling fortnight-long festival of fun and debauchery, no doubt encouraged by the licentiousness of the masked disguise. It was probably no wonder the Austrians outlawed the Carnevale in 1797 and it did not re-emerge as an annual event until some two centuries later in 1979.

Glamour vs Melancholy

The game of concealment and revelation is intrinsic to Venice. However, so too is the concept of the gaze, fittingly epitomised by the mirror, a luxury chattel for which the Venetians were duly famed. In the 16th century the island of Murano, long revered for its skillful glass production and invention of crystal glass, developed revolutionary flat-mirror technology applying an amalgam of mercury tin to create silver mirrors. These bespoke mirrors, created with a dusting of gold leaf and bronze, were renowned for their ravishing reflections. Lured by the mirrors' lustrous enhancement, the nobility of Europe treasured them as highly prized objects of desire, unperturbed that they may cost as much as a ship. Given their importance to the economy and in order to preserve technique, the Murano glassmakers were not able to travel beyond the city and had to keep their methods secret upon penalty of death.

Inside the fine palazzos of Venice, beautiful mirrors still stand proud, their now-speckled black and silvered surfaces poignantly reflecting the glamour of Venice past. A sense of melancholy, visible in touches of elegant decay, is most acutely invoked by the centuries-long decline in population affecting the timbre of the community; *La Serenissima*'s end, the second plague, the ravages of 20th-century war and the incursion of 530+ cruise ships per year have all played their part. The beguiling cityscape of *centro storico* certainly continues to weave her dream-like charms. However, the population of approximately 30,000 residents, at a third of its peak, is now entirely focused on the tourist economy, endangering the inherent spirit and vivacity of Venice and inducing a certain wistfulness.

When struck, these melancholic chords reveal the complexity and sophistication of Venice. In harmony, they meld past and present together in the one moment, awakening our emotions and provoking our intellect, evincing a visceral experience, a gift from one of the world's most human of cities and one that should inspire hope for its future.

'In Venice one must succumb to delicious unknowingness, for you will find unexpected things to fuel your imagination and stoke your soul.'

Navigate

Venice Today

No matter how well you prepare for being on the ground in Venice, I have one critical thing to divulge – you will still get lost! There is nothing to do but surrender yourself and embrace chance and mystery in a world afflicted by information overload. Succumb to delicious unknowingness, for you will find unexpected things to fuel your imagination and stoke your soul.

'One of my favourite things about Venice is arriving by water taxi through Burano and bursting into the Grand Canal.'

Rachel Griffiths

Sestieri

You know when you can't see the woods for the trees? Well the map of Venice has always appeared before my eyes as a bit of a jumble, distinguished most clearly by the Grand Canal curling its way through the lagoon like a cascading ribbon. That was until I was prompted to contemplate the *centro storico* as a fish…and lo and behold, there it was. Why not equip yourself too with this visual cue as it will undoubtedly expedite your understanding and your navigation of Venice as you journey through its ancient quarters.

The Laguna Veneta, sitting just off the Adriatic Sea is peppered with more than a hundred islands. Venice, as the largest landmass, is also the most orderly and compact of cities, comprised of six districts, hence their Italian descriptions as *sestieri*, from *sesto* or sixth. These sestieri had their beginnings in the 12th century.

Cannaregio:
the crown

Santa Croce:
the gills

San Polo:
the pectoral fin

Dorsoduro:
the jaw

San Marco
the abdomen

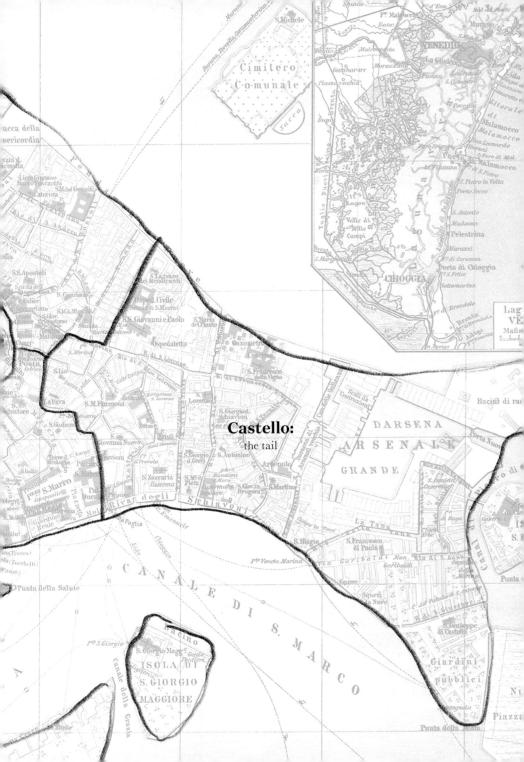

Castello:

the tail

Cannaregio: the crown

Cannaregio's name reflects its ecological heritage with *canna* meaning cane. No longer a reed-filled swamp, Cannaregio is one of the most sizeable neighbourhoods of Venice. Its accessibility and proximity to all forms of transport including Venezia Santa Lucia, the island's station, can make staying there advantageous, especially if arriving into Venice late or leaving Venice early.

The bustling Strada Nuova extends from the station to the Rialto Bridge and then to St Mark's. In peak times it hosts a relentless flood of tourists and the proliferation of shops and venues catering to this crowd can lead to dismissive opinions of Cannaregio. However, it is simply that its charms are not so immediately obvious.

Once you deviate from the well-trodden path and head northwards you will find the oldest Jewish ghetto in the world. Originating in the 16th century, the buildings are clearly distinguished by their unusual six- and seven-storey height, necessary for a crowded enclave where physical restrictions were imposed. The Museo Ebraica de Venezia together with businesses and restaurants associated with Jewish life ensure a good balance is struck between its historical past and its culture today. This is also true for much of the residential areas with daily produce markets and choice eateries and wine bars found along streets such as Fondamenta Misericordia.

A notable trio of churches in this sestiere – the Gothic Madonna dell'Orto, the Renaissance period Santa Maria dei Miracoli and the arresting Santa Maria Assunta, known as *I Gesuiti*, after the Jesuits who had the church built, continue to attract visitors.

Dorsoduro: the jaw

A respectable parade of grandiose palazzi grace Dorsoduro's concise exposure along the Grand Canal. However, a predominantly relaxed and low-key vibe permeates this sprawling district, due in no small part to the presence of Ca'Foscari University.

This also might be why the area hosts not only the classic museums of Gallerie dell' Accademia and Ca'Rezzonico, but less traditional museums, with the Peggy Guggenheim Museum making its home here. In the last decade joining the ranks was the Punta della Dogana, the latest contemporary juggernaut from luxury brand supremo, Fraçois Pinault.

The area is known for having a good range of restaurants, especially those catering to the hip pocket of students, as well as a livelier nightlife, particularly around Campo Santa Margherita. Happily for those seeking a more authentic culinary experience they need only find the Accademia Bridge to lead them to their next food adventure.

On Dorsoduro's southern side, the generously proportioned Fondamenta affords peaceful, uninterrupted views across to the island La Giudecca, best appreciated on sunny days strolling, gelato in hand, or whilst enjoying a sunset aperitivo. A view appreciated too, by the billionaires on their super yachts anchored at the AAA mooring near the eastern tip of the sestiere.

Santa Croce: the gills

At the entrance to the Grand Canal, along its southern edge is Santa Croce, named after a monastery demolished in 1810. Santa Croce's strength lies not so much in its 'must sees' as in its layout, which encourages wandering through its unpredictable pathways, imparting a degree of immersion and a peek into the rhythm and spirit of a Venetian locale.

Change and Venice are not often included in the same sentence. However, this sestiere has been the poster child for Venetian projects in the 20th century ignited by Benito Mussolini's commissioning of Ponte della Libertà. This bridge has linked the island to the mainland and thereby Santa Croce's territories include Piazzale Roma, followed by the manmade island of Tronchetto and now the Cruise Terminal. The recent addition of the People Mover (light rail) has further enhanced linkage and access. It is significant infrastructure indeed and a likely facilitator of the tourism onslaught of recent decades. Santa Croce is certainly the entry point into Venice for the wheel-heeled.

VENICE KNOW HOW

Venice has its own idiosyncratic numbering system that does not begin and end in the one street but is often continuous, snaking around corners and across canals. The methodology seems unclear and it is a maze all of its own.

•

Do not expect the numbers to be joined to a street name.

San Polo: pectoral fin

Settled around the 9th century CE, San Polo is one of the oldest parts of Venice together with San Marco, which it is joined to via the Rialto Bridge. Named after the Church of San Polo it is also the smallest quarter sporting many narrow *calli* perfect for discovering the more curious and intimate boutiques and artisan businesses nestled between the ever-multiplying souvenir shops.

San Polo flourished during medieval times as a kind of mercantile mecca; not only were the food markets sited there, prestigious banks were also ensconced around Rialto, as were the workshops of the top goldsmiths. The commercial heritage is ever present with the famous fish markets continuing the legacy, beckoning the locals with their catch from the Adriatic and shops tantalising visitors with their special wares.

Also located in this area is the renowned Scuola Grande di San Rocco, which boasts the most important Tintorettos in the world.

VENICE KNOW HOW

Along the course of one street its name may change several times.

•

GPS is great but ancient Venice can bamboozle even 21st-century technology.

•

Locations of *campi, ruga, calle* and so on are characteristically indicated by black lettering upon a white oblong background, called *nizioleti*, meaning 'little sheets', as in bed sheets.

San Marco: the abdomen

Originally named Rivoalto, for a millennium San Marco was the political apex and the district from which *La Serenissma* governed and built her empire. No longer a seat of power, the sestiere remains the beating historical and cultural heart of Venice. Piazza San Marco is the jewel in the city's crown with world famous vistas across the lagoon to Isola di San Giorgio Maggiore and San Salute. It is here that royalty alighted from their ships, where criminals were punished, enemies vanquished and victors exalted. In modern times the Carnevale uniquely commands this space in a celebratory fashion. The Venetians have long been masters at the art of the spectacle.

This district harbours a hit parade of Venetian experiences: the Palazzo Ducale, Basilica di San Marco, the Ponte dei Sospiri (Bridge of Sighs) and the famed La Fenice opera house to mention just a few, so it is no wonder that visitors are held in its thrall. As the *numero uno* sestiere for all, it is perhaps unsurprising that this showpiece area has the smallest number of residents and therefore limited range of local services. Being so thoroughly imbued with historical spirit and gravitas, it somewhat suppresses the organic evolution of a contemporary soul. Instead, San Marco adheres to Venice's most bedazzling and alluring mode; elegant, luxury boutiques grace Calle Larga XXII Marzo and nearby are most of Venice's 5-star hotels, including the renowned Hotel Bauer (see page 161).

Castello: the tail

Castello has a yin and yang quality. As daytrippers depart from Piazza San Marco they often surge towards the promenade-worthy Riva della Schiavoni. However, after their seventh large footbridge they usually tire of venturing further and retreat. This might be a secret weapon of the Venetians as it seems to cure tourist curiosity, leaving the westward sector to the inhabitants. Eastwards from the Giardini Pubblici towards the island of Sant'Elena it becomes a far quieter and genuinely neighbourhood affair with peaceful walks under the parasol pines of Parco delle Rimembranze and views of modern-era apartment buildings.

The Giardini, created in the Napoleonic era, and the magnificent Arsenale situated in Castello constitute the two principal Biennale venues. The 12th-century Arsenale is a living testimony to the Empire's naval power and might. It is an extraordinarily impressive set of old shipyards and armory buildings to view and experience. That being said, any semblance of pomposity and grandeur is nullified by the spectacle of the laundry suspended between residences in nearby streets.

'Art world insiders
and glamour junkies
alike stress that
the water taxi is the
only way to arrive
in Venice.'

Arriving in Venice

Air

Ok, you have your entire luggage, hat, jacket and bag all delicately balanced and you are champing at the bit to be in Venice's magical orbit. All you need to do is turn left out of Marco Polo Airport and follow the sheltered walkway for about 750 metres. At the end of this sometimes sweat-inducing, wobbly-wheeled jaunt you will find the private water taxis and *vaporetti* (public water buses), which will whisk you away to the island of Venice and her nearby isles.

ATVO TREVISO AIRPORT

Treviso Airport largely services intra-European destinations as well as low-cost airlines including Ryanair. The airport is only 42 kilometres from Venice and the most direct way to connect with Venice is via bus or taxi.

Water

Could there be a more enchanting and fitting way to arrive at the lagoon than by boat, lightly bouncing over the waves with the occasional spritz of seawater upon your face? Of all the options, this is by far the most arresting, atmospheric and inspiring way to enter this sensual city.

You will have been told that tickets are available through various means, but be warned, every time I arrive I am greeted by a different booking permutation – from payment at an airport desk, to a booth by the water taxi…or pay the driver directly once inside the boat. If you are looking for absolutes, forget it, you will need to readjust and just go with the flow. Rest assured, in Italy it always works out – served with a modest dose of chaos and a tonne of charm. Oh, and even though credit cards are accepted, make sure you have some cash on hand…just in case.

Water taxi

Art world insiders and glamour junkies alike stress that this is the only way to arrive in Venice. Cast aside your scepticism; let's remember that these special creatures are captive to beauty and adept at seeking and seizing the experiential moment.

VENICE KNOW HOW

Private water taxis start at 110 euro
for up to 4 people. Beyond that, it is
11 euro per person. The taxis can carry
up to 10 people so with more aboard it
becomes a compelling marriage of
glamour and economy.

•

A small reduction applies for return journeys.

•

Water taxis are available for bookings at
all hours – especially helpful if, as once
happened to me, your plane is delayed till
2 am and no public transport is available.

•

They offer door-to-door service
to many 5-star hotels.

Vaporetto

For those who are prioritising a diminutive footprint rather than the ticking clock, then the water bus, also known generically as the *vaporetto*, is just the thing – and with pennies potentially saved, might allow for a blowout on Bellinis.

The Alilaguna water bus runs several lines that ferry you away to the major Venetian destinations including San Marco, Fondamente Nove and Rialto, along with the main islands of Murano and Lido.

Validate your ticket on the electronic readers before hopping on the *vaporetto*.

•

Always purchase a ticket (*biglietto*) from the conductor as the fines can be hefty without one.

Linea Blu is the all-rounder line servicing 12 destinations including Murano (30 minutes), Fondamente Nove (41 minutes), San Marco (90 minutes), Giudecca Stucky (103 minutes) and the Cruise Terminal (110 minutes). Departures are every half hour.

Linea Arancio solely services Venice Island, tick-tacking across the Grand Canal attending to eight destinations including Madonna dell'Orto (30 minutes), San Stae (50 minutes), Rialto (56 minutes) and Ca'Rezzonica (65 minutes). Departures are every half hour.

Linea Rossa is the fastest line to San Marco clocking in at 72 minutes but beware, it is seasonal running only from April–October. A trim line with only 5 stops including Murano (30 minutes), Lido (60 minutes) and Giudecca Zitelle (80 minutes). It runs on an hourly schedule.

For more details see alilaguna.it/en

VENICE KNOW HOW

It is worth taking the time to study the map of Venice carefully. You may find that there is more than one *vaporetto* stop that is near your point of departure/arrival – it may simply entail a bit of street navigation to locate it.

•

Similarly, sometimes it is easier and faster to walk rather than take a ride.

Vaporetti allow for one bag (150 cm in total) before potentially charging a supplement. Plus it's physically demanding transferring luggage from a bobbing pontoon onto a boat with your balance and dignity intact.

•

Deposito bagagli: Help is at hand. Luggage storage is available at Marco Polo Airport, Piazzale Roma, Venezia Santa Lucia and the Cruise Terminal, and also offered by a few private operators in town. Make sure you are aware of their opening hours. There is also a luggage deposit in front of Hotel Canaletto, Castello (veniceluggagedeposit.com).

Wheels

If the road is your chosen path to Venice and you are happy to park romance until you arrive in *centro storico*, then the 35-minute taxi or bus ride from the airport, only 12 km away, is for you.

For those who have their own wheels then there are a number of parking options:

1. Piazzale Roma is on the doorstep of the Grand Canal, however, close proximity also translates into high demand and slow-moving traffic. In high season, Piazzale Roma can present a busy and challenging environment.

2. Tronchetto, a manmade island, is slightly further afield, but can be preferable to Piazzale Roma, especially during peak periods. A shuttle train, known as the People Mover, takes just a few minutes to get you to Piazzale Roma. Tronchetto is the most amenable, accessible and largest parking option.

3. Mestre, only a few kilometres away on the mainland is another alternative, and allows for a quick getaway when leaving for other destinations. There are several parking companies that, dependent on their location, allow for the option of a quick bus trip transfer into Venice or a short train ride across the lagoon to Venezia Santa Lucia in Venice's Cannaregio district.

Bus

From Marco Polo Airport, you can hop on one of two buses. The Venezia Express coach operated by the regional bus company, ATVO, is the more comfortable and faster choice of the pair.

Simply exit the airport through Door D, turn left and head to stop no.2.

Tickets cost 8 euro each or 15 euro return and can be purchased a multitude of ways.

Further details at atvo.it

Aerobus is a commuter bus operated by Venice's public transport company, ACTV, so your luggage may compete for space with passengers. The upside is that there are a greater number of stops that are pertinent if your accommodation is on the way. Other advantages include a smooth transit from bus to *vaporetto* if you choose to purchase the combo ticket, Aerobus + Nave for 14 euro.

Exit the airport and look for the ACTV bus stop. Take the no.5 bus.

For more details on ACTV products and timetables see actv.avmspa.it

Taxi

If communal road transport does not fit the bill, then a taxi from the airport will take about 25 minutes and the fare is approximately 60 euro.

TRAGHETTI

Traghetti are gondolas that operate solely for convenience rather than pleasure. It is handy to keep the traghetto in mind when you want to traverse the Grand Canal without one of the city's four bridges in sight/reach or the desire to zig-zag in a vaporetto. The trip takes only two minutes for 2 euro and it is the tradition to stand. Keep your eyes peeled for one of the seven somewhat discreet stations when you want to save your legs and your time.

Tracks

Cheers to the inventor of the train – so human, so civilised. What other mode of transport, that runs at fast speed, without requiring any steerage from you, so seamlessly transfers you smack bang into the heart of town?

Venice has two train stations or *ferrovie* – Venezia Mestre and Venezia Santa Lucia. Venezia Mestre located on the mainland is a major hub. It takes a mere 12 minutes to journey from here to Venezia Santa Lucia, which is a terminus.

Venezia Santa Lucia, established in 1860, is located in the *centro storico* and is named after the church that once stood there. Venezia Santa Lucia's modernist building is a reincarnation that had its beginnings in 1924 with architect Angelo Mazzoni but was continued in tandem with Virgilio Vallot and finally completed in 1952 under Paolo Perilli. It has the honour of being one of the few 20th-century buildings in Venice.

To avoid confusion and distinguish the stations from one another when making bookings, I think of M for Mainland and therefore Mestre.

BIGLIETTI

Train tickets and reserved seat bookings can be made at selected travel agents throughout Venice – offering advantageous savings on time and effort. There is one near Hotel Londra Palace, San Marco.

Dream

Inspirational Places
for Creatives

Venice knows how to put on a feast.
Its churches and museums, with their
mélange of influences from the nexus of
Eastern and Mediterranean trade, have
imbued the city with a sumptuous heritage.
These receptacles of culture, designed by the
lauded architects of the day, and redolent
with paintings, sculptures and frescoes have
long been cherished by the cultured traveller.
However, in recent times there have been
fresh places set at this banquet of art and
choice has expanded from the classical
to embrace the wave of contemporary
foundations and museums opening their
doors in the city.

Museums

Ca'Pesaro
SANTA CROCE

The metaphysical master Giorgio de Chirico never fails to garner attention for *Il Trovatore* 1950, a feature work within the handsome collection of 19th- and 20th-century European art housed in the Baroque palazzo of Ca'Pesaro. Gustav Klimt's *Giuditta II* (Salome) 1909 and Marc Chagall's *Il Rabbino di Vitebsk* 1914–22 invariably capture visitors' admiring gaze, and are striking acquisitions for the Gallery of Modern Art that owes its establishment to a number of generous benefactors, beginning with Duchess Felicita Bevilacqua La Masa who gifted the building to the city in 1898. It soon became a treasure house founded upon art that had been acquired at the second *Esposizione Internazionale d'Arte della Città di Venezia* (Venice Biennale) in 1897.

As you glide through the galleries designed by the master Venetian architect Baldassare Longhena, keep your eyes peeled for the transgressive and slightly unsettling visages by Post Impressionist sculptor Medardo Rosso, the charming *La famiglia Guidini* 1873 by Giacomo Favretto, Felice Casorati's curious *Le Signorine* 1912 and Antonio Donghi's *Donna al caffè* 1931, a fine work that relates to the period's topical *Neue Sachlichkeit*, or New Objectivity.

Complementing Ca'Pesaro's permanent display is a rotating calendar of temporary exhibitions, often in dialogue with aspects of the collection to prompt deeper reflection and enhance the experience. A Museum of Oriental Arts occupies the top storey of the palazzo. It boasts a significant collection of Japanese art from the Edo period, bequeathed to the city over a century ago by Prince Henry of Bourbon-Parma, Count of Bardi.

capesaro.visitmuve.it

Ca'Rezzonico
DORSODURO

A museum dedicated to the age of splendour, dissipation and decadence – something every fine city should have, no? It features three core collections with the transposed Ai Do San Marchi Pharmacy on the top floor, keeping them quirky company.

The palazzo was originally commissioned in the 1640s by the Bon family, but both financial hardship and the death of architect Baldassare Longhena meant that it took another 80 years and the design of Giorgio Massari to complete it for the next owners, the Rezzonico family.

The Browning Mezzanine, (named after famous onetime resident, the poet Robert Browning) features the Ferruccio Mestrovich Collection comprising 30 paintings that span 500 years, with the core focus on Venetian art of the 15th to 18th centuries including notable works by Jacopo Tintoretto. On the next two floors remarkable 18th-century furnishings, tapestries and art are in full flight with four rooms sporting ceiling frescoes painted wholly or in part by Giambattista Tiepolo. A most splendid example celebrates a Rezzonico marriage in the aptly named Nuptial Allegory room. More joys await with early views of the Republic by Canaletto, the only such works owned by the city, and a room decorated with Pietro Longhi frescoes.

Amongst one of the most significant bequests to Venice is the scholarly collection of Egidio Martini who possessed an astute eye for hitherto unknown and underappreciated artists (mostly Venetian) from the 15th century onwards. The collection, on display since 2001, has been a valuable resource for academics leading to significant advances in knowledge of the period.

carezzonico.visitmuve.it

Museo Correr
SAN MARCO

Situated within the golden precinct of Saint Mark's, but at its furthest point, is Museo Correr, a museum that quietly devotes itself to telling the story of Venice's art history and culture. It owes its name to the art collector and noble Teodoro Correr (1750–1830), whose collection formed the basis for the institution.

The Wunderkammer section reconfigured in 2013, houses treasures from the city's past with 300 works drawn from the civic museum's collection including Jacopo de' Barbari's famous view of Venice, dated 1500. On the first floor are the Neoclassical Rooms dedicated to the Republic's celebrated sculptor Antonio Canova and decorated with frescoes by artists including Giuseppe Borsato and Pietro Moro. A further 20 rooms focus on Venetian life across themes ranging from the Doge and governance, artisanal guilds, the judiciary, numismatics, cartography, festivals, games, militaria and maritime power.

More awaits the visitor with the elegantly furnished nine-room Imperial apartment offering an intriguing insight into the sumptuous style to which the Austrian Empress Sissi, who lived here for some months in 1862–63, was accustomed. Upstairs the Pinacotheca section focuses on *La Serenissima*'s impressive artistic legacy, fittingly featuring the Venetian Bellini family of artists, but also extending to Flemish painters with Pieter Brueghel the Younger's *Adoration of the Magi* c.1600 a highlight. Keep an eye out for the striking 15th-century *Portrait of a Young Man* thought to be by Antonio Leonelli da Crevalcore, a member of the hugely influential Ferrara School.

In recent years the museum has undergone a noticeable acceleration and expansion of its exhibition program with shows traversing a wide spectrum of culture often in collaboration with prestigious international institutions and private collections. For instance: *Spheres of the Heavens, Spheres of the Earth* 2008; *800 Unpublished Drawings from the Venetian 19th Century* 2010; *Gustav Klimt in the Sign of Hoffmann and the Secession* 2012; *Fashion Vocations: Agatha Ruiz de la Prada* 2013; *LEGER 1910–1930 A vision of the contemporary city* 2014 and *Jenny Holzer. War Paintings* 2015 a collateral event presented in the 56th Venice Biennale. Also of note was *Lucian Freud* 2005 an exhibition that still, to this day, conjures marvellous memories.

The Correr is one of Venice's largest museums and its spaciousness and scale has the added benefit of being less crowded, a retreat from the bustle of the tourist zone outside its door with a welcome café on site.

correr.visitmuve.it

When in Venice, artist Sally Smart
always makes a pilgrimage to the
Accademia to behold Vittore Carpaccio's
Storie di Sant'Orsola (The Legend of Saint
Ursula) 1490-98, a cycle of nine paintings.
Of the luminous and highly symbolic
The Saint's Dream, Smart comments:

**'I adore this painting – note the
little dog and slippers, layered
with symbolism, quite surreal with
odd distortions and atmosphere.
Strange and familiar, it's a
beautiful dreaming painting.'**

Contemporary artist and scholar of Renaissance painting, Aida Tomescu, is enthralled by the vast riches of the Accademia, visiting there most days in the last 90 minutes before closing, especially during the Biennale, as it affords a greater chance of quiet and contemplative space as visitor numbers dwindle.

She recommends 'bite-sized visits' to counter being overwhelmed, and for those short on time to head directly to Room 10 to view great works by Tintoretto, Veronese and especially Titian's *Pietà* 1575.

On this Aida reflects:

'Titian lived to a very old age – the Venetian archives list him at around 102 but it is believed he greatly exaggerated this and may have been in his late 80s or his 90s when he painted the *Pietà*. The breathtaking scale of the work, nearly four metres high, for a man of his age is in itself incredible. Intended always for his tomb, the *Pietà* was left in his studio at his death in 1576. I take great heart in knowing that Palma il Giovane, the young painter who undertook its completion, understood Titian's untamed creativity and left most of the work in the hands of the master.'

Gallerie dell'Accademia
DORSODURO

Situated in the former convent of Santa Maria dell Carità resides a roll call of Venetian masters from Giorgione to Tintoretto, Veronese, Bellotto and Canaletto alongside precious works from the Byzantine and Medieval eras. In addition to the vast permanent collection, the Accademia has long played a critical role in the restoration of art and until 2004 the art school, the Accademia di Belle Arti di Venezia, occupied the same premises. Temporary exhibitions contribute to the institution's calendar, however the gallery's website is almost as antiquated as the art itself, so go old school and just turn up and enjoy what befalls you.

gallerieaccademia.org

Palazzo Mocenigo
SANTA CROCE

This museum celebrates costume, both the outward appearance of clothing and the unseen accompaniment of perfume. Imagination and pleasure are sparked by the display of 17th- and 18th-century patterned dresses adorned with lace and finely embroidered silk waistcoats for gentlemen. Also explored is the tradition of perfume used to scent rooms, clothing, gloves and the nobles themselves. It seems appropriate that this alchemical practice formed an important commercial proposition for the mercurial Venice.

Palazzo Mocenigo presents a place to satisfy those yearning for a tactile and sensory experience that involves more than the eyes.

mocenigo.visitmuve.it

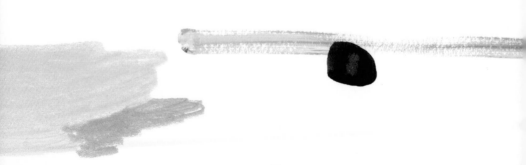

54

Palazzo Grassi and Punta della Dogana
SAN MARCO AND DORSODURO

Luxury goods magnate and Christie's auction house proprietor François Pinault is the pin-up boy for contemporary art in Venice. Following the inception of Pinault's palaces, three foundations also opened their doors in the city. This über-collector is either prescient or powerful or both. Either way Venice and art followers should recognise Pinault's lead in re-invigorating and re-contextualising the city's long-abiding relationship with art, which has catapulted it into a shining contemporary beacon.

Palazzo Grassi was the last Republic-era palazzo to be built along the Grand Canal (it was completed in 1772) but it was the first of Pinault's suite of cultural venues and is his most classic. Exhibitions of works from Pinault's immense and impressive collection encircle the perimeter of the three-storey central atrium, offering multifold views. Palazzo Grassi opened in 2006 and three years later was joined by Punta della Dogana, the more physically arresting of the two museums, bordered by the waters of the Giudecca Canal on one side and the Grand Canal on the other.

Since 2013 weekly talks, screenings, theatrical performances and concerts have been offered by Teatrino di Palazzo Grassi, the third cultural venue to have benefited from restoration under Japanese architect, Tadao Ando's balanced and restrained sensibility tempered with a dose of dramatic flair.

palazzograssi.it

Museo Fortuny
SAN MARCO

Mariano Fortuny was a polymath who revolutionised set design and stage lighting and whose repertoire of talents encompassed textile design and the invention of tripod floor lamps. Over 60 years ago his wife Henriette Negrin endowed the city with Fortuny's collection of fabulous wall hangings, paintings, photographs and stage sets. The museum masterfully stages exhibitions against a backdrop of sublime interiors that artist Rosslynd Piggott describes as belonging to an 'extraordinary and rarefied world'.

Magic transpires on the first floor where the salon walls are bedecked from ceiling to floor with Fortuny's fabrics, with not a sliver of light to behold, and considered curation places objects and paintings in subtle relationships with one another. These rooms cocoon and blanket the mind transposing the individual towards the cusp of an intoxicating dream-like state – an engrossing visceral and intellectual experience. Without a doubt, it tops my list of favourite house museums, anywhere.

The palazzo's location is tricky to find and it is only open when an exhibition is running. With accessibility proving at times to be elusive, Museo Fortuny is the ultimate art insider's museum.

fortuny.visitmuve.it

'The inventive curatorial programs within this beautiful, multi-storied Gothic building in Campo San Beneto, make it a beautiful mix of old and new Venice. It never disappoints.'

Tony Ellwood, Director,
National Gallery of Victoria

Peggy Guggenheim Collection
DORSODURO

Possessing a killer location on the Grand Canal is Peggy's Palazzo Venier dei Leoni. This unusual single-storey building sports a 'secret' rooftop terrace with knockout views where, from a *vaporetto*, you might spy the Biennale crowd enjoying a sunny spring brunch or a wedding party drinking in the spectacular sunset views with cocktails in hand.

The intimacy of this museum is conveyed through the nature of the collection and the physical proximity visitors are accorded in viewing the art. The walls whisper Peggy's story and through the vanguard artworks you can sense the vibrations of her relationships with artists. The collection, weighted towards American and European Modern art, fairly covers the breadth of 20th-century 'isms' and always looks fresh with loans adding light and shade.

It's easy to immerse yourself in the collection enhanced by the cool, elegant space and on each visit I personally feel compelled to pay homage to Constantin Brancusi's *Bird in Space* 1932–40 and delight myself once more with a view of El Lissitzky's Suprematist painting *Untitled* c.1919–20. Not to be overlooked, the temporary exhibitions presented in a second building directly across the shade of the Nasher Sculpture Garden tease new perspectives on the modern masters.

The museum is a testament to the avant-garde queen's status as an art icon but also her influence on cultural memory. Given the affection Peggy Guggenheim invokes amongst art aficionados, it is no wonder that the collection tops many Venice lists.

guggenheim-venice.it

Foundations

Fondazione Emilio e Annabianca Vedova
DORSODURO

In a space designed by Renzo Piano, Fondazione Vedova supports a program of studies, conferences, scholarships and exhibitions in its aim to promote the legacy of leading 20th-century Venetian, Emilio Vedova's art practice (1930–2006). Exhibitions are oriented around Vedova's core theme of 'painting-space-time-history', which often places his work in a discourse with other international artists.

fondazionevedova.org

Fondazione Prada Venezia
SANTA CROCE

In 2011, Ca'Corner della Regina, once the property of Pope Pius VII, became the Venetian presence for the Fondazione Prada, which had been inaugurated almost two decades earlier. The Foundation supports an ongoing program of restoration for the palazzo whilst holding annual exhibitions that intelligently interrogate culture, flexing the eye and the mind. This museum of ideas was joined by a second venue for the Foundation's impressive conceptual vision with the opening of the capacious Milan premises in 2015. Respect should be paid to an organisation that has a Thought Council within its ranks.

fondazioneprada.org

Fondazione Querini Stampalia
CASTELLO

The last descendent of the Querini Stampalia family generously opened the doors to his ancestors' personal history when he instituted the Foundation in 1868. This celebrated house museum reveals not only the art, furnishings and accoutrements of its patrician inhabitants amassed over 400 years, but it also has extended the span of the collection with bequests and donations from artists including pioneering conceptual artist Joseph Kosuth.

A major feature is the beautiful library that provides an engaging study environment and is open to all as part of the Foundation's cultural mission. In the 1960s Carlo Scarpa was commissioned to restore parts of the palazzo and his magic touch extends to the garden, which should not be missed. More recently, architect Mario Botta has orchestrated a clever synthesis of historical and new elements into the building imbuing it with a contemporary flavour.

querinistampalia.it

Fondazione Giorgio Cini
CANNAREGIO

Inaugurated in 1951, the Giorgio Cini Foundation's twin mission was to restore and resurrect the island of San Giorgio Maggiore and its Benedictine Monastery after 150 years of military occupation and to establish a cultural centre emphasising Venice's legacy. This initiative has met with great success and it now also hosts the Vittore Branca Centre, which allows scholars and artists to research the collections and libraries of the Foundation to study the cultural history of Italy. Check the website for upcoming events such as concert performances from the resident scholars.

cini.it

Espace Louis Vuitton
SAN MARCO

A more recent addition to the Foundation family, Espace Louis Vuitton has partnered with the authority Musei Civici di Venezia and committed to restoring important Venetian works. Renowned contemporary artists are subsequently invited to engage with the restored heritage work as part of the Foundation's desire to spark links between past and present. The fruits of the forged relationship are exhibited during the Biennale season.

eu.louisvuitton.com

Museo Ebraico di Venezia
CANNAREGIO

A petite museum that casts a light on Jewish life and history in Venice that began more than 600 years ago. In exchange for the granting of freedom to practise their faith and for protection from the Republic, the Jewish people were obliged to live in a quarter known as a *ghèto* – Europe's first ghetto. The five synagogues in this condensed part of Venice attest to the ethnic and social diversity within the Jewish population, with the German, Italian, Canton, Levantine and Spanish congregations each having its own Scuola.

museoebraico.it

Churches

San Zaccaria
CASTELLO

Sam Chatterton Dickson, Sales Director of
one of the first international contemporary
art galleries London's Lisson Gallery, cites
Giovanni Bellini's *San Zaccaria Altarpiece* 1505
as his favourite painting in Venice, if not in the
world. Keep some coins handy (a mere 50 euro
cents) to illuminate the paintings and assist
funding restoration work.

Basilica Santa Maria Gloriosa dei Frari
SAN POLO

Another cherished haunt of Sam Chatterton
Dickson conceals some wonderful works of
art behind its Gothic doors, amongst them
Titian's first significant commission, reputedly,
at the tender age of 24, the beautiful *Assumption
of the Virgin* 1516–18. Titian's compositional
treatment of the Virgin depicting her as smaller
in comparison to the foreground figures at the
time was considered radical. Whilst he upset
the friars it cemented the artist's reputation and
ultimately the painting became the most famous
in the city. Venice's largest Gothic cathedral
also features one of Giovanni Bellini's finest
works, *Madonna and Child* 1488 which you may
enjoy beholding during Mass if you are unable
to visit during the short opening hours.

Scuola Grande di San Rocco
SAN POLO

This building contains the most significant collection of Tintoretto paintings in the world. It took almost a quarter of a century for the artist to complete his commission to create a cycle of narrative paintings for the walls and ceiling of three halls and the altarpiece. Keep an ear out for concert events as there are few better, more beautiful ways to experience the art than with the accompaniment of music.

San Giorgio Maggiore
CANNAREGIO

Former Venice Biennale commissioner and philanthropist, Simon Mordant recommends bucking the trend by travelling in the direction of the popular gaze directly across the lagoon from San Marco to the church of San Giorgio Maggiore. Designed by acclaimed Neoclassical architect Andrea Palladio, it boasts works by Tintoretto and Jacopo da Bassano and inspiring views from the campanile.

Santa Maria dei Miracoli
CANNAREGIO

Marvel at the architectural presence of this precious polychrome marble Renaissance church which was built on the 'reverse' premise, to house a tiny painting of the Madonna believed to be imbued with miraculous powers.

Isola degli Armeni di San Lazzaro

Artist Rosslynd Piggott suggests visiting this Armenian monastery on an island, established in the 18th century at the site of a former leper colony (c.12th century). 'It is a strange and ancient world still functioning just a short distance from the Lido. It houses a treasure trove of ancient manuscripts, paintings and artefacts, so precious that Napoleon dared not touch it.' There's a guided tour each afternoon; visitors must join the tour to visit.

Cattedrale di Santa Maria Assunta
CANNAREGIO

Pre-dating the Basilica di San Marco, this
medieval church on the island of Torcello
is, in Rosslynd Piggott's words, 'desolately
beautiful, solemnly spiritual'.

Isola San Michele

The peace, solemnity and timelessness of
this cemetery island are the perfect remedy
for Jan Minchin, Director of Melbourne's
Tolarno Galleries, when she wishes to completely
remove herself from the art rumble. A place
of transcendence and respect.

VENICE KNOW HOW

Venice has 139 churches, all of which have
different hours of opening, so make sure
you plan ahead to avoid disappointment.

•

Buy a Chorus Pass for single entry across
different days to 18 churches of note.
An individual pass is 12 euro, available
at participating churches or online at
chorusvenezia.org, which also offers tours
and advises of upcoming concerts as well as
opening times. This excellent initiative is
convenient, economical and most importantly
supports the much needed and ongoing
restoration of the city's other
museums, the churches.

'Apart from all the wonders in Venice, I do love to visit one of my favourite artists, Vittore Carpaccio. And of all his works, the splendid *St George and the Dragon* 1516 in his desert lair, the landscape littered with parched bones and body parts (quite gruesome) and little lizards in the foreground.'

Sally Smart

My Perfect Venice Day

The advancing march of contemporary art has injected the floating city with a shot of cultural vibrancy. Venice clearly spans the archaic to the anarchic and in typical 21st-century fashion the old world now frames fascinating dichotomies such as the intimacy of the Peggy Guggenheim Collection vs the grandeur of Museo Correr and the gravitas of the Gallerie dell'Accademia vs the punchiness of Punta della Dogana.

As contemporary art sets my heart and mind aflutter, if I only had one day I would choose to spend it at the Punta della Dogana then Fondazione Prada Venezia.

For those like my grandmother, Lorli, who are classically inclined, I would suggest a visit to Gallerie dell'Accademia and then stopping in at Fondazione Querini Stampalia.

Revel

The Ultimate Art Experience

Often described as the Olympics of the art
world, the Venice Biennale is the *numero uno*,
the most prestigious, and the granddaddy of
biennales. Indeed, it is a spectacle that transfixes,
interrogates, catalyses thought, and immerses
the individual in a sensory wonderland. Days
are required to de-compress and decode the
wave of intense and voluminous art; rogue
fragments sometimes emerge from the depths
of my subconscious months later. Ultimately,
while the art elite power through it in three days,
for everyone else the Biennale is a splurge of art
and culture for all, spiced with lusty dashes
of food and fun.

History of the Biennale

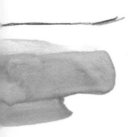

A progressive desire to create a fresh international forum for contemporary art as well as to celebrate the silver wedding anniversary of King Umberto I and Queen Margherita di Savoia, led to the launch of I Esposizione Internazionale d'Arte della Città di Venezia *(1st International Art Exhibition of the City of Venice) in 1895.*

Set in the verdant Giardini di Castello in a building designed by Enrico Trevisanato, this first incarnation of the Biennale d'Arte met with instant success, its exhibition of Italian and European artists visited by 200,000 people. In less than two decades Belgium established the first international pavilion and was swiftly joined by Hungary, Germany, Great Britain, France and Russia. Now, more than 120 later, art junkies surpass the half million mark and the scope of participants has moved beyond a Eurocentric emphasis to embrace countries that include Mongolia, Kuwait, China, India and Angola. The event features a remarkable 89 nations with 30 historic pavilions occupying the precious soil in the Giardini and the remaining nations exhibiting in palazzos, churches and quirky venues throughout the city. Anchoring the event is the singular vision of the Curator along with the adventurous spirit and maze of Venice enmeshed in the event's cultural web.

How to Tame the Biennale Beast

One arrives for the Biennale armed with curiosity, enthusiasm and a burning desire to seize it with both hands; but its scope, content and even its layout are unimaginable. Hence, the need for a toolbox equipped with insight and insider experience to tackle the challenges that lie ahead.

BIENNALE KNOW HOW

The Biennale d' Arte occurs in odd years and the Architettura in even years. Both run for six months from May to November and are open Tuesday–Sunday from 10am to 6pm.

Twenty-nine national pavilions occupy the Giardini della Biennale. Most are flag bearers for Europe, but new world countries like the United States, Canada and Australia, and Asian compatriots like Japan and Korea have also staked their claim.

The Venice Biennale is a mercurial beast that escapes a prescriptive and definitive itinerary by virtue of its temporal nature. So in the absence of being able to advise you to 'make sure you visit the mind-blowing James Turrell light installation' or 'see this or that particular masterpiece' we should instead turn to the structure and framework for the event. Think of the Biennale as a house supported by four pillars, starting with the themed international exhibition devised specifically for that edition by the Biennale Curator. Sharing an equal load are the representative nations who proudly push the button on their cultural message within their own pavilions. The next two pillars are the associate collateral events and the institutional exhibitions from the local Venetian museums.

Now Venice may be small when it comes to cities, however it has a magical ability to compact art into virtually every corner. With so much to see, how do you untangle a plan from all the confusing and competing threads? How do you wrangle the beast?

Vernissage

If this sophisticated word is not in your regular lexicon you can be forgiven, for it is usually only bandied around by the art crowd. Whilst is certainly conjures a certain *je ne sais quoi*, it merely refers to a launch event. Derived from the French word meaning 'varnishing' it was applied in the 19th century to refer to the day before an Art Salon exhibition where the artists added the final touch of varnish to their paintings. Canny collectors soon realised that this was an opportune time to view and secure new works and started visiting and buying on 'varnishing day'. Over the years, the Vernissage has come into wider circulation and is code for the preview period for an event that tends to infer invitation only.

In the case of the Venice Biennale, it takes the shape of a three-day private preview period for the art mob who from Wednesday to Friday traverse the vast array of venues and attend the best parties of the season.

AUSTRALIA

**Andrea Cashman, Director at
David Zwirner in New York, is a Vernissage
veteran. Here she shares a typical day:**

'When I'm in Venice I wake up early – I like to give myself enough time to walk everywhere and that means factoring in some extra time for inevitably taking a wrong turn somewhere. I love getting lost in Venice!

Most often I will meet a curator or a client for breakfast and we will make an itinerary together. Day one of the Vernissage usually starts with the Arsenale since I usually have at least one artist there and it tends to set the tone for how I digest the Biennale as a whole. Ideally you have a full day to do the Arsenale and to spend time with the work and really immerse yourself in the videos, but there is a lot of socializing that happens too. I usually have at least three espressos per day and rarely stop for a proper lunch.

Dinner is usually a party for a specific pavilion. Sometimes this means that a gallery has rented an incredible palazzo and you get to see a private part of Venice.'

From Giardini to Arsenale

As the Biennale is spread all throughout the island, prioritising the pillars is the first step and this means focusing on the two prime and essential locations – the Giardini della Biennale and the Arsenale. While the exhibitions of each edition refresh each time, the 'G' and the 'A' remain the heartland and main stage for Biennale activities. The Giardini hosts dozens of countries with one super-sized Central Pavilion dedicated to the official theme ordained by the über-Curator. Their vision takes flight on a mind-blowing scale throughout the Corderie section of the Arsenale. In recent years newcomers from other countries have succeeded in finding lodgings towards the behemoth's rear and the Ministry for Cultural Affairs has established the *Padiglione Italia* (Italian Pavilion) for showcasing Italian art.

BIENNALE KNOW HOW

The first pavilion was built in 1907 and the last to receive a precious plot of land from the Commune di Venezia was Australia who erected their building in 1987 and then rebuilt it in 2015. No more pavilions can be granted land here now.

Each nation typically presents a solo exhibition by an artist or collective. The method by which the artists are chosen for this prestigious honour varies but commonly countries appoint their own special committee who undertake an exhaustive artist selection process, around 18 months before the Biennale opens.

One of the curious peculiarities of exhibiting in Venice is that everything must be transported on barges. This does limit the scale and weight of certain artworks, particularly in the discipline of sculpture.

The Central Pavilion, formerly known as the Italian Pavilion, is the largest building in the Giardini. It boasts a vast array of rooms all dedicated to showcasing artworks chosen by the Biennale curators in the service of their themed vision.

By comparison, the supporting players are more disparate in their location, the collateral events hosted in all manner of buildings that change from year to year. It is not at all unknown for these satellite events to surpass pavilion exhibitions and you certainly should be encouraged to seek these out as part of your itinerary. Venice's museums never lag in the quality of their exhibitions but at Biennale time they seem to lift again. Researching reviews online is the wisest strategy to know how to plan for these associate chapters or seeking out the opinions and advice through trusted word of mouth.

Armed with some perspective on the Biennale format, how do you best tackle the event itself on the ground? Well, you truly need a minimum of three days to attempt any meaningful encounter with the art and culture of Venice, Biennale season or not. Beyond that, it is really a matter of which lifestyle attitude propels you that will determine the intensity of itinerary. Given that time, energy, distance and mental concentration are your core considerations I would recommend one major activity per day for the languid, two for the buoyant, and mmm…the occasional three for the devilishly driven/FOMO/art obsessive, although I would warn that it's extending ambition to its very edge.

VENICE KNOW HOW

For those attending the Biennale's three-day party-rama, also known as the Vernissage (or befittingly a voyeurs-age), there will be a cavalcade of glorious events to attend…or possibly crash. Glamour is essential and high-heels for women and elegant footwear for men are non-negotiable once the sun sets. While appearances count, savvy women never toss practicalities aside, always having a pair of ballet flats at hand for transit (trust me, you will be thankful when you are stumbling around cobblestone *calli* in the moonlight trying to retrace your steps to your abode and momentarily hostage to the city's labyrinthine nature).

Biennale Itinerary

Day One

A.M.
Giardini della Biennale

Seize your first taste of the Biennale in the pleasure gardens. Zipping between art and nature, immersed in the intellectual and the visceral, what's not to love? How many pavilions is it possible to view in a morning? Well, some will take five minutes and others could enchant for an hour. Probably the best part of a day is required to see every single country and it is debatable whether that includes the Central Pavilion (see page 80), which can easily chew up a few hours alone. On this count, it may be beneficial to make a return visit.

P.M.
Punta della Dogana

After dashing between countries in the Giardini, pull up anchor at the restored 17th-century Customs house, Punta della Dogana – François Pinault's second contemporary museum space in Venice after Palazzo Grassi. The exhibition is likely to feel positively restrained and sparse after the carnival of aesthetics and concepts in the Giardini. Pritzker Prize–winning architect Tadao Ando's design riffs on a raw vs smooth play, positioning exposed brick walls alongside his signature concrete: a material nod to the interweaving of old and new. The free-flowing spaces provide a beautifully calibrated arena in which to contemplate the thoughtfully curated exhibitions drawn from Pinault's collection. Pause at the chic cafe set within the bookshop for a timely refuel and refresh with a *spremuta d'arancia* or an excellent coffee and cake.

Day Two

A.M.
The Arsenale

The Arsenale – a massive and manifold chamber of secrets that is best tackled when you are fresh. Occupying some 50,000 square metres, this major Biennale site is particularly demanding on both the mind and the body, so it's wise to decide whether you want to go hard and dedicate a major slice of your day here or gently engage and absorb it in two halves.

P.M
Peggy Guggenheim collection

The intimate scale of Peggy Guggenheim's palazzo and her museum filled with mid-century art provides a beautiful and calming counterpoint to the spinning energy and enormous scope of the Arsenale. This early forerunner of the flourishing private house museum model belongs to the modest, non-grandiose style where the art commands attention and takes centre stage rather than the architecture, pretty as it may be.

An alternative, if you are in need of a leave pass from art, is to escape to the Lido – a 10-minute *vaporetto* ride from the Giardini della Biennale stop on Linea 5.1. Ride a bike along the foreshore, take a dip and enjoy being under the open warm skies. Or if lunch in a garden of Eden is desired then glide across the lagoon to Locanda Cipriani on Torcello island.

ARSENALE KNOW HOW

Your last challenge here is to circumvent backtracking through the Arsenale and you can do this one of three ways:

•

1. Hot foot it back to the main entrance by walking down the perimeter path that skirts the Arsenale's walls. This takes about 10–15 minutes from beginning to end and passes by the amenities and a handful of food and beverage facilities.

•

2. Leave via an exit at the base of the Giardino delle Vergini and walk across the Ponte dei Pensieri into the streets of Castello.

•

3. Nab a *vaporetto* at San Pietro di Castello (line 4.1 and 5.1; closest drop-off stops are Ospedale and Fondamente Nove).

Day Three

A.M.
Museo Fortuny

Museo Fortuny is an utterly lustrous jewel in Venice's crown. You must not miss the sheer joy of visiting one of the most fascinating and elegant house museums in the world. Bravo to the intelligent and inventive exhibitions that spark intriguing associations and dialogue between Fortuny's collection and the curatorial interventions.

P.M.
Giardini/Arsenale and/or collateral event

Perhaps a return visit, at a leisurely pace, to one of the two principal Biennale spaces to fill in the gaps especially as video work is likely to feature prominently. Alternatively, hone in on a sestiere in which to explore collateral events and non-Giardini pavilions that have received good reviews. (Post-Vernissage verbal reports, blogs and media will start publishing their recommendations – use these to cut to the chase).

NOT FOR SALE

In response to political protests staged by students at the 1968 Biennale, who were upset by the commercialisation of the art world, two years later the Biennale organisers closed the sales office, which had been operating since the Biennale's inception. Instead they chose to reposition the event with a curatorial thrust, cannily appointing highly regarded curators for a single biennale to present their own narrative alongside the individual exhibitions of each participating country.

Since then, sales have migrated to a different sphere and post-Vernissage, enthusiastic collectors simply hook up with the artists' representing commercial galleries in order to strike a deal.

Art Insiders' Itineraries

Simon Mordant

The former Australian Biennale Commissioner advises to 'Pace yourself – you can't possibly see everything on a first visit'.

Day 1
Visit 'the Giardini', as the art crowd refers to it, otherwise known as the Giardini delle Pubblica or the Giardini della Biennale.

Day 2
Head to the Arsenale.

Day 3
Visit the Foundations, where they usually hold excellent international exhibitions to coincide with the Biennale.

Day 4
Spend the day in the churches with an art historian to guide you through the treasure trove of religious buildings where art, design and music are in full magnificence.

Day 5
Take a boat out to Murano and Torcello and simply wander.

Rachel Griffiths

The actor, director and advocate keeps it streamlined and in sharp focus.

Day 1
Head to the Giardini and see as much as possible then grab a sandwhich.

Day 2
Back to the frontline again for Giardini Part 2.

Day 3
Go hard in the Arsenale and then enjoy a well-deserved long lunch at Corte Sconta in Castello.

Georges Petitjean

The Curator of the Museum of Aboriginal Art, Netherlands recommends three days as a good starting point, but five if time is on your side.

Day 1
Start at the Giardini, which contains about 30 national pavilions.

Day 2
Allow one full day for the Arsenale. If time allows, you can always return to the nearby Giardini to visit (or revisit) national pavilions.

Day 3
Visit the several pavilions spread around town. This is an excellent way to discover Venice itself. You will discover palazzi and other buildings as you wander down hidden and quaint alleyways.

Days 4 & 5
There is a difference between the official Biennale venues (national pavilions) and collateral events. Spend your last two days visiting these collateral events/exhibitions, which are sometimes in magnificent edifices like Palazzo Fortuny.

The Artist Experience

Without artists, there is no Biennale. And without an artist's perspective, this book would skirt the fringes of aberrance and discordance, denying a valuable and refreshing insight. With this in mind I've approached three international artists whose arresting, intuitive and intelligent presentations have seared themselves into my memory as some of my favourite Biennale moments.

Nathalie Djurberg and Hans Berg

Artist Nathalie Djurberg won the prestigious 2009 Silver Lion award for promising young artist for her wildly immersive and striking multimedia installation *The Experiment*. Her towering and bright floral sculptural garden punctuated with darkly humorous and transgressive characters wrought in claymation was deeply compelling, as was the abstract, evocative, hypnotic music created by her partner and collaborator, Hans Berg. Here, Nathalie shares stories from her and Hans's Biennale adventures.

How would you describe Venice?

We went in February to see the location and be shown around, that was our first time in Venice. It was flooded and empty and foggy, incredibly beautiful. People drank coffee while sitting with water up to their ankles, or even up to their knees in some cafes. That elicited a sense of doom that the world was surely coming to an end – but first an espresso! And smirks if you order a cappuccino at the wrong time of the day, which is any time after lunch.

Beyond the major museums, do you have any tips for hidden or off-the-beaten-track must-sees, cultural or otherwise?

No, since we have been there so little we don't remember any street names or places. We were lost all the time and everything was fascinating.

How would you describe your experience on the 'inside' as an artist producing work and being at the Biennale ?

Installing the show was chaotic but really nice. We did everything up until the end, where it turned out we didn't have enough lights. We had ordered new lights and they came at 11pm the night before the opening, but we had no cables for them. Then we got amazing assistance from some of the guys working there. Before, it would have been impossible to get even a broom or vacuum cleaner, but at this point of panic, we got incredible help, and the guys worked until 4am.

The entire process of making a work for the Biennale was fantastic. Daniel Birnbaum (the Biannale Curator that year) and curator Jochen Volz gave us all the freedom. No censoring, just leaving us in peace making the work. And stupidly, I made all the sculptures in a small studio in my apartment, where the studio room wasn't enough, so the entire apartment was the studio for half a year.

Any other general tips to offer about Venice?

Don't stress, just walk around and have a Spritz.

Patricia Piccinini

In 2003 Patricia Piccinini presented *We are Family* in the Australian Pavilion. Her phantasmal sculptural beings and vehicular creatures centered on her interest in scientific concepts and the ethical implications and interventions made possible by genetic engineering in our technology driven world. The Biennale garnered widespread acclaim for her work and led a young Piccinini to exhibit in institutions, Biennale and commercial galleries around the world. Here, Patricia shares her Biennale memories.

Beyond the major museums, do you have any tips for hidden or off-the-beaten track must-sees, cultural or otherwise?

As someone with young kids I'm always looking around for something that I can do with them outside of the art world, but that is still interesting. We are quite fond of the Museum of Naval History, which is very old school – full of dusty wooden scale models of boats and ships and the like. It might be in line for a renovation but I hope they don't change it too much.

How would you describe your experience on the 'inside' as Australia's representative artist at the Biennale?

The 2003 Venice Biennale was one of the most intense experiences of my life, highs and lows and just like being carried along by a hurricane. The installation period was just wonderful. Of course, it was often difficult. Doing anything practical in Venice is always unexpectedly complicated, and most requests are met with a response that begins with 'Well, the problem is…'. However, I had a fantastic group of people all working towards this unknown moment just up ahead. I had never been to the Biennale before the one I was in, so I had absolutely no idea what to expect.

When it hit, the Vernissage was like a four-day tornado of meeting, eating and interviews – I think I did 80 press interviews. No time for looking at art, or even thinking, but the response was so amazing. And then, just as suddenly, it was over. In those days everybody headed straight to Art Basel directly after the Vernissage so the whole thing seemed to stop so abruptly it was shocking. It was like you woke up and there were tumbleweeds rolling through the Giardini and you're left with this post-euphoric slump wondering what just happened.

Years later I still feel the positive effects of that show. I've just come back from Brazil where my show at CCBB (the Cultural Centre in Brazil) has toured to four venues and been seen by over a million visitors, and the curator of that show saw my work in Venice 13 years ago.

Do you have any general tips to offer about Venice?

We always stay in an apartment and tend to cook for ourselves; the markets are great and there is only so much restaurant food I can take. Queuing with the nonnas for prosciutto and stracchino at the Casa Del Parmigiana is both an achievement and a joy.

We always try to stay in Castello, ideally close to Piazza SS Giovanni e Paolo. It's in between our two main Venetian interests, the Rialto Markets and the Biennale, it's reasonably quiet without being a backwater and you can get from the airport and back quickly and economically on the Alilaguna ferry.

Shaun Gladwell

2009 marked an auspicious year for Shaun Gladwell, who represented Australia at the Biennale with his dramatic and commanding series MADDESTMAXIMVS. Gladwell, known for his multi-disciplinary practice, focused on how the body moves through space and time. Framed initially through urban expressions of his generation such as skateboarding, BMX bike riding and beatboxing, he extended his 'performative landscapes' to outback settings.

Here, London-based Gladwell reveals his thoughts on the city not designed for wheels.

What do you love about Venice?

I love the graffiti around the old fish markets in Rialto, that's kind of one of the moving postcards of the city that I always track. I also love that modern banking started in that area of Venice considering modern banking is still the bane of my existence, but I think its great to know where it started from.

As a skateboarder, I love this great Italian city even though it's one of the worst cities for skateboarding, mainly due to the cobblestone roads and the fact that most of the streets are actually canals.

However, there is a good skate place off Via Garibaldi, it's the biggest open space in Venice for street skateboarding and freestyle skateboarding. If you are a skateboarder having withdrawals you have to head there for the most beautiful skateboarding spot in a generally un-skateable city.

Where do you frequent when you're in town?

I go to Harry's Bar, which is a famous watering hole in Venice, and try to settle down. I am privy to the seats that Ernest Hemingway would always sit at. I always try to take those Hemingway seats and sit and think about life in general and how exciting it is in Venice.

As for accommodation, my recommendation is The Gritti Palace. It's just a couple of thousand euros a night, which is not so bad, and you can get a water taxi directly from the hotel on the Grand Canal, which will be so overpriced that it will make you almost fall into the canal itself! But if you don't want to spend a few thousands euros you can just go there for breakfast, which is actually what I usually do no matter where I am staying. It's an amazing breakfast, it is still quite overpriced, but it is the most spectacular breakfast I have ever had in my life. Eating on the Grand Canal watching all those *vaporetti* and gondolas and other watercrafts floating both ways from the lagoon right through to the Rialto Bridge is stunning.

Biennale Checklist

Whether you are attending the Vernissage or visiting the Biennale on any of the other 197 days of its existence, the following practical words of advice might help ease your way.

Survival kit

Firstly, before embarking on daytime adventures consider assembling a survival kit: water bottle, a snack, Band-Aids, a map…and then add GPS, lip balm, an ACTV Vaporetto pass and a scarf to counter temperamental weather (virgin wool or a cashmere–silk mix will suffice, but do not even dare to pack a plastic poncho – practical but so unchic!). A few useful and polite words of Italian would also not go astray. Yes, it sounds reminiscent of a hiking kit, however, only if you have made the fashion faux pas of carrying it in a rucksack. No – your deluxe survival kit is best tucked into a fabulous designer version in leather, or slipped discreetly into one of the de rigueur canvas totes that swing nonchalantly from your shoulder.

Why bother with such a kit, you may ask? If you are really committed to culture, earthly needs such as bandaging blistered feet and eating lunch are not high on the radar; surely feasting on art provides sufficient sustenance for the soul. On a more prosaic level, food venues in the Giardini and Arsenale are not plentiful and their queues often long in the peak viewing times. Hopping between Biennale venues whilst fun sometimes feels akin to a complicated cross-stitch; including some snacks in your kit alleviates the blood sugar dive that inevitably occurs at the moment you are lost, frustrated and failing to see the surrounding beauty. Food cures all! I also find a quick stop for an espresso gets the blood pumping again and kicks concentration back into gear.

Tickets for the Biennale, post-Vernissage, can be purchased online or on site at the entrance to the Giardini and Arsenale. They start at 25 euro per day and Permanent Passes are available too for unlimited entry. Cast your eye over the official website for details of regular and any extended opening hours as well as information on upcoming collateral events and the like.

labiennale.org/it/arte/

General checklist

- Fashionable yet truly comfortable shoes as you will be clocking the miles across relentless swathes of concrete, stone and pebbles. Soft runners, ballet flats and wedges of any style are favoured by women, and for men, style meisters might opt for designer high tops, loafers, designer sneakers or similar.

- Platform sneakers are particularly handy to cope with the city's unpredictable and intermittent H_2O moments and flooding tendencies.

- Amenities/survival kit

- An old-school map for when the GPS fails

- Patience for when you inevitably get lost (likely to be a daily occurrence)

- Humour – for the above

BIENNALE KNOW HOW

If you feel overwhelmed and possibly afflicted by art overdrive – it's time for a Spritz.

•

Remember – you will never get to the end of the Biennale rainbow; it keeps its shine through the perennial possibility of more discovery around the corner.

•

Clocking the miles between exhibitions is a welcome activity, offering relief as it gives you space to digest.

•

It is unrealistic to expect the vision of the Biennale Curator to be fully sustained across all exhibits, so temper expectations and look for the gems. If you can name at least three you are doing well.

'Mind-blowing contemporary art surrounded by some of the oldest historic buildings on the planet today, Venice is just so vivid and intense in this way! Murano is always an absolute standout for me and I have so many art highlights from the Biennale: the life-changing Henri Rousseau show, Fiona Hall in the Australian Pavilion, Sarah Lucas in the British Pavilion... I could go on and on.'

Del Kathryn Barton

Transcend

Beyond Venice

While there is no doubting Venice's magnificence, there are moments when you might wish to wrench yourself from its clasp, regroup and refresh by switching terrain and tempo. A day trip to one of the outlying islands such as Burano or Murano may prove to be the tonic, or you might choose to reconnoitre further afield towards the mainland. There are also other destinations within reasonable reach sans airport transfer. There are myriad options – but here is a snapshot of a handful of propositions all within a few hours of Venice.

Day Trip

Burano, Murano, Torcello

Travel editor Susan Kurosawa recommends
Burano, 'home to traditional lace-makers and
unfurling canals; and sister island to Murano,
the isle of glass blowers' for a short day trip. Both
are a short *vaporetto* ride away (around 45 minutes
from San Zaccaria, near St Mark's). In Burano,
Susan recommends Ristorante-Enoteca Riva
Rosa for lunch. 'The Ammendola family opened
the pink-painted Riva Rosa as an adjunct to their
nearby lace-making atelier and shop where for
three generations the finest tableware and bed
linens have been made on site. Riva Rosa has
umbrella-shaded outdoor seating and a menu
that emphasises the seafood of the immediate
waters, from grilled scampi and spaghetti tossed
with briny little clams to its signature dish of
baked salt cod casserole, which comes with a
crust that is cracked open, the fish filleted and
served at the table with near-operatic ceremony.'

isoladiburano.it
rivarosa.it

Brenta Canal and Veneto Villas

Unbeknown to many, it is possible to continue inland by boat beyond the waterways of Venice. If you are headed to Padua, why not consider journeying along the Naviglio del Brenta, or Brenta Canal, where you can gaze at the impressive 15th- and 16th-century villas that border the canal, many designed by the architect of the day, Antonio Palladio. These summer residences for the Venetian glitterati and titans of the Republic were built upon former medieval farmlands. No longer were the elite grazing on the fruits of their land but were also gazing upon Tintoretto and Veronese, the fruits of their success.

You can book a day-long mini-cruise along the canal aboard a comfortable river barge (see page 101), with three villa visits included and an option for lunch, or else you can go rogue and bring a picnic or visit one of the cafes along the way.

The most outstanding villa on the Brenta is the Villa Pisani offset with stunning gardens designed by Girolamo Frigimelica de' Roberti. This unabashed symbol of power comprises 114 rooms built to celebrate the appointment of Alvise Pisani as the 114th Doge (1735) of Venice. Lavishly decorated, most notably with an enormous ceiling fresco by Giambattista Tiepolo: a modest proposition titled the *Glory of the Pisani Family*. However, with the fall of the Republic, the shine rubbed off the Pisani fortunes and in 1807 they were compelled to sell the ultimate Baroque trophy home to Emperor Napoleon. He was said to have spent only a few nights there, but his resident stepson remodelled and added the Napoleon Apartment replete with his accoutrements and canopy bed. Seven years later it was transferred to the House of Habsburg, continuing its history of illustrious ownership.

Now a museum, some 30 rooms are open to the public, it also hosts exhibitions and a cafe, for a brief respite after strolling through the beautiful gardens and maze. At the end of the day, it's just a 30-minute trip by train back to Venice.

ilburchiello.it

Luxury on the Brenta

Those who seek a more luxurious way to explore the surrounds of Venice might be swayed by the idea of a river cruise ship. Certainly, in recent years the word 'ship' has struck a discordant note as Venice has become beset by serious and potentially damaging issues relating to the impact of large cruise ships. This has created opportunities for compact river-based ships that pride themselves on their comparatively small footprint. One boutique operator has tapped into the market for the art-inclined and environmentally conscious traveller by offering culture-oriented itineraries that extend beyond Venice and Padua to Bologna, Verona and Milan (via a combination of waterways and road), amplifying the theme by decking out their ships with a curated collection of fine art.

uniworld.com

Silversea

Fancy your own butler on your Mediterranean voyage to Venice? Silversea spoils guests with one-to-one crew attention on their ultra-luxury ships. Intimacy and mindful engagement are also hallmarks of Silversea who consciously keep their ocean ships small by industry standards with only 300-500 guests on board. They also offer an extended overnight stay in Venice.

silversea.com

Padua

Said to be northern Italy's earliest city, Padua, with its close proximity to Venice, makes the perfect one-day adventure, or conversely a base from which to make day trips to Venice.

A clear favourite of many an art insider when I surveyed my confrères for viewing recommendations was Padua's Cappella degli Scrovegni. This single-nave church features astonishing frescoes painted by Giotto (1303–05) representing three story cycles related to Christ, the Virgin Mary and Joachim and Anna set against an ultramarine blue background – it's somewhat akin to being locked inside a jewel casket.

Owing to the frescoes' fragile state it is essential to book tickets before you visit, either online or from your hotel, a minimum of 24 hours in advance, as visitors are limited to 25 per session on a timed entry. Fifteen minutes are allocated to the climate-controlled chapel itself and another fifteen to a multimedia room. For the passionate Giotto follower a quarter of an hour may be tight, so you could try to book sequential sessions to seize a bit more time in heaven.

Padua possesses other charms making a short stay a serious consideration; there is the petite but enchanting Orto Botanico di Padova, the world's oldest academic gardens (1545) created by Daniele Barbaro, where many exotic species sourced through Venice's trade relations were grown and studied.

Admire the architecture of one of Italy's oldest seats of learning and a leading centre of humanism and the sciences, the University of Padua. It earned its first historical mention in 1222 and counts Nicolaus Copernicus among its alumni and Galileo Galilei, who chaired Mathematics, as a luminary of its academic staff.

Or why not simply stroll around the narrow streets engaging in Padua's rich history, which included rule under the Romans, Goths and Lombards with a gelato in hand and let time slip calmly by.

Overnight

Transit Farm

This Italian fashion house doesn't just dress you for holidays, it can take you on one. Transit Farm, located in the Breganze hills of Veneto only 90 minutes from Venice, takes its lifestyle vision a step further. The designers of clothing label Transit Par Such have over 5 years with 9 full-time artisans reinvigorated a handsome, classic two hundred year old farmhouse hewn from stone and wood to create a place that articulates the language of spartan elegance with lashings of rustic chic.

Two apartments, accommodating two to four people, serve as a great base for exploring the surrounding area. Make your way to Asiago and pick up some traditional alpine cheese and tasty speck, then head to Bassano del Grappa where in season you will find creamy white asparagus, before a last stop at Marostica to nab a punnet of their cherries. Nestled back at your apartment select a vino bianco from the farm's own vineyard and cellar door and dip bread in the olive oil from their grove. Or if a dinner party is on the agenda then Transit Farm can arrange for private chef to whip up a storm whilst you enjoy the house prosecco in the 'relax' room on the Kenzo designed sofas. Next morning, embark on your own walking tour to see the stables and delight in the sight of the fine horses bred on the property, or take some riding lessons from one of their professional trainers.

Transit Farm also offers a wine cellar open to the public where wine tours and tastings are available for its four BIO varietals that include Vespiaolo, Merlot and the regional speciality, Torcolato.

transit.it/farm

A hidden treasure only five minutes drive from Transit Farm, Villa Godi Malinverni was the first villa designed by the Renaissance's most influential architect, Antonio Palladio. Completed in 1542, it is set amongst beautiful gardens and boasts classical frescoes by artists including Battista del Moro and Gualtiero Padovano. It also features the quirky Pierluigi Malinverni Fossil Museum founded in 1852, the same year that marked the local discovery of fauna and flora fossils. After touring the property, you might consider a meal at the on-site restaurant Il Torchio Antico.

Further afield

MILAN

Where there is wealth, art and culture tends to follow and Milan, only two and half hours by train from Venice, does not disappoint with a legion of museums and cultural experiences on tap. It certainly does not need to begin and end with its most famous feature, Leonardo da Vinci's *The Last Supper*, incredible enough as it is.

MILANO - Il Duomo

Pinacoteca di Brera

Treat yourself to an amazing in-depth collection of Renaissance art with an emphasis on religious subjects at the esteemed Pinacoteca di Brera. Open to the public since 1809, its artworks date back as far as the 14th century, many from former churches. Highlights include Piero della Francesca's *The Virgin with Child, Angels and Saints* 1472–74 known as the Brera Altarpiece, Caravaggio's *Supper at Emmaus* 1606 and Andrea Mantegna's sublime *The Dead Christ and Three Mourners* 1470–74, which intrigues with its unusual compositional perspective, ethereal nature and pathos.

You also have the rare opportunity to witness conservation in real time as a painting enjoys painstaking attention from conservators in white coats encased in a glass box. This great initiative known as both the Visible Museum and the Restoration Laboratory started in 2002 and has become an integral part of 'the Brera' experience. Keep a half-day spare if you want to visit all 38 rooms of this grand dame, it offers an old-school education and window into the past that only a legendary European institution can provide.

pinacotecabrera.org

Museo Poldi Pezzoli

In the 1930s my family lived in Milan and the museums and art galleries were an immense source of delight to my Italophile and art-educated grandmother. One of her favourite haunts was Museo Poldi Pezzoli, which she considered a gem amongst Europe's house museums.

RITRATTO D'INCOGNITA · Pier-della Francesca
Milano. Museo Poldi Pezzoli
1428 – 1498 ·

The nobleman Gian Giacomo Poldi Pezzoli started his own house museum in 1846, built upon an inheritance that he substantially expanded, eventually leaving his legacy, upon his early death in 1879, to the Accademia di Belli Arti (Brera Academy) of which he was a patron.

Pezzoli commissioned interior designers Luigi Scrosati and Giuseppe Bertini to create an array of spectacular rooms inspired by the historical past to display his prized collection of armour and weaponry, applied arts, jewellery, furniture and art. Paintings from northern Europe including Lucas Cranach's *Portrait of Martin Luther* c.1529, complemented his works from the Italian Renaissance. His collection was notable for its commitment to Lombardian artists to demonstrate his civic patrimony, as Giovanni Battista Moroni's *The Knight in Black* c.1567 attests.

Museo Poldi Pezzoli affords a fascinating view into an era and style of collecting fuelled by a particular kind of privilege, passion and perspective that no longer exists. Peel yourself away from the sartorial temptations of Via Manzoni and acquaint yourself with one of Milan's best-kept secrets, located just near La Scala.

museopoldipezzoli.it

Fondazione Prada

As you stand at the imposing gates of Fondazione Prada, moments before opening time, it's as if you are anticipating crossing the threshold into Willy Wonka's factory where your reward awaits. However, this time the golden ticket is larger than life – a gold leaf building, a 'temple' to the permanent collection's artworks by Robert Gober and Louise Bourgeois. Nicknamed the 'haunted house' this is just one of the seven monumental buildings, both new and recalibrated from their days as a distillery (established in 1910). A chic industrial vibe is at play with Rem Koolhaas's firm OAM embracing the prevailing industrial grey of Milan but offsetting it with carefully considered touches of orange, glass, mirrors and the aforesaid restrained gold bling. It's an engaging dialogue between materials, light and reflection. Prada and Koolhaas have created a quietly dramatic and understated complex that manages to elegantly dazzle – so very Milanese.

The premises occupy a whopping 19,000 sqm imparting enormous scope and latitude for exhibiting the permanent collection, special temporary exhibitions and support for a range of multidisciplinary events, some of which take place in the onsite Theatre.

The foundation steers itself away from overtly prescriptive museology practice, more interested in offering a cultural complex that will prompt, probe, ponder and spark curiosity and lead to discourse. Its beliefs are squarely centred on the transformative powers of culture and the foundation has expressed this in part through its initiative directed at children, the Accademia dei Bambini, which presents weekend workshops devised by educators, artists and scientists driven by a cultural-pedagogical focus.

Here, subtlety pervades yet surprises are still to be found through the discovery of obscure connections and juxtapositions. For instance, the toilets located below the entry foyer are reminiscent of the gridline framework for a 1980s analogue video game; a real need set against a surreal and suspended reality.

Bar Luce, the Wes Anderson–designed cafe is a jaunty contrast to the complex's largely austere tonal palette. Exuberance abounds with Formica tables and furniture in tutti-frutti pastel pink and mint green dancing upon a playful terrazzo floor accompanied by jukebox tunes. It's a complete shift in cadence and harks to the transformative post-war era, the 'economic-miracle' when Italy became an industrial powerhouse and many fortunes were made and undoubtedly through which this Foundation and this art centre were made possible.

Is a former industrial site an appropriate venue for high-falutin' contemporary art? Yes, indeed, it is the very foundation in every sense of the word.

fondazioneprada.org

Milan's contemporary gaze

Francesca Minini

Gallerists Francesca and Alessandra Minini have art in their blood: a father who has long been a renowned and successful contemporary art dealer in Brescia. They have forged their own path, establishing a Milan gallery in 2006. Initially their program was mostly focused on Italian art but soon expanded to include international artists including Ghada Amer, Dan Graham, Ali Kazma and Matthias Bitzer. An interest and passion for spatially conceptual work unifies their gallery vision curated with much thought and finesse.

francescaminini.it

Massimo de Carlo

De Carlo is the big cheese in town. After more than three decades, his art empire now extends to London and Hong Kong, fuelled by his powerhouse stable of contemporary artists that runs the gamut from young guns like Elad Lassry to the rock stars Maurizio Cattelan, Urs Fischer and Carsten Höller, testament to de Carlo's serious chops.

massimodecarlo.com

Galleria Lia Rumma

A gallery distinctly flavoured with artists from Arte Povera and Conceptualism, realms to which it committed itself back in 1971 when it first opened its doors with a space in Naples. Instrumental in discovering, introducing and nurturing some of the protagonists of these important art movements, the gallery's impressive rollcall features a cavalcade of first-generation representatives; think Marina Abramovic, William Kentridge, Joseph Kosuth, Haim Steinbach and Anselm Kiefer. Lia Rumma balances the mix well with the next generation, which includes Vanessa Beecroft and Marzia Migliora who hold true to the original premise of the gallery.

liarumma.com

Kaufmann Repetto

'F' does not only stand for 'fashion' in Milan, but also 'feminism' with another sister force on the art scene. Francesca Kaufmann and Chiara Repetto's gallery program is calibrated towards the video and installation spheres with a particular dedication to young female artists. Renowned South African multi-media artist, Candice Breitz spearheads the female charge, which Kaufmann Repetto have steered across the Atlantic into a second space in New York.

kaufmannrepetto.com

Fondazione Nicola Trussardi

Not to be overlooked is Milan's other resident foundation, Fondazione Nicola Trussardi, which was brought to life in 2003. This nomadic, dynamic and plastic institution invites artists to conceive and create contemporary art projects and works for exhibition within and across Milan's historical buildings and civic spaces, to support, promote and disseminate cultural discourse through contemporary art that is confronted with the city's layered past. It is not averse to partnering with major international institutions such as Tate Modern, London – a smart move to reach a broader audience and to more widely transmit their cultural message and grant more ambition and scale for artists to execute grand visions.

fondazionenicolatrussardi.com

Unmask

Venice's Most Interesting Mercantile Delights

Once renowned for its artisans,
its guilds and its sparkling mirrors,
Venice now glints and glistens more often
from camera flashes and visitors' bling.
Calli once punctuated with leather ateliers
and boutiques flaunting their lustrous wares
have been buffeted by the winds of change,
depleting or banishing these businesses
already engulfed by souvenir shops.

Clothing & Style

It is not only the encroachment of tourist wares eradicating the artisanal personality of the city; extravagant window displays attest to the stealth march of the luxury labels, slapping another layer of 'beige-wash' on Venice. This engenders a pronounced fragility to that precious space 'in-between' keenly sought by the aesthete; meaning the bespoke, the uncommon, the quintessential, the beautiful, the singularly Venetian. Such things tend to represent an antithesis to the bland uniformity and the accelerated tempo that exist now in our material and increasingly monotone world.

Thankfully, in hidden pockets and even in plain view, gems survive – in fact thrive – in spite of the sightseer culture that continues to surge into Venice with unrelenting force. Some things are always valued and forever timeless in this ancient and intimate city.

In your art-free moments, enjoy these pleasures of another kind shared by urbane *cognoscenti* along with my friend Marita Lillie, part-time resident of Venice, artist and fashion maven, whose family's superfine wool is woven into the garments of the major Italian fashion houses.

WOMEN

Pot-Pourrì
SAN MARCO

Pot-Pourrì beckons seductively with its artful vignettes of luxurious wares. A sense of timelessness pervades its two lifestyle stores in Venice with their beautiful clothes and homewares. Quality is the guiding principle with cashmere, silk, fine cotton and leather across a range of innately stylish labels from Robert Clergerie and Sofie D'Hoore to Napoleone Erba, complemented by their own in-house collection of knits, coats and accessories.

Venezia Fashion
Palazzo Regina Vittoria | Ramo dei Fuseri 1810

Venezia Home Lifestyle
Palazzo Regina Vittoria | Frezzaria 1820M

potpourri.com

MEN & WOMEN

La Coupole
SAN MARCO

This high-end purveyor of cool threads has 'his and hers' stores as well as a store for baby fashionistas. It spans the luxe spectrum, with classic Italian labels such as Armani and Versace dazzling just as brightly under the light bouncing off the Murano chandeliers as the newer and edgier labels.

Men & Women
Calle Larga XXII Marzo | San Marco 2366

Baby
Frezzeria | San Marco 1674

Al Duca D'Aosta
SAN MARCO

An upmarket boutique with a decidedly urban groove and understated sophistication, Al Duca offers an array of accoutrements from labels including Brunello Cucinelli, Belstaff, Comme Des Garçons, Lanvin Paris, Isabel Marant, Marni, Moncler and Theory. The business had its beginnings as a men's shirt-fabric shop in 1902 and prides itself on reinvention and delivering up-to-the minute catwalk collection looks. This applies to the digital world too, with Al Duca D'Aosta offering online shopping.

Calle Larga XXII | San Marco 284
alducadaosta.com

Transit
SAN MARCO

No one does casual, urbane and discreet sophistication better than the Italians and Transit is particularly masterful at this style. The label distinguishes itself by its commitment to beautiful fabric treatments and a subtle palette from which it extracts the most sublime and delectable shades of colour...rarely repeated, but always nuanced so that the tones harmonise across the seasons. And yes, I am a Transit devotee.

Calle dei Fabbri | San Marco 4673
transit.it

ACCESSORIES

Michele de Fina
SAN MARCO

Contemporary flair meets classic tradition in chic leather goods. A sweeping sculptural line and a hand stitching 'motif' distinguish this covetable, modern range of handbags, briefcases, wallets, belts and silk scarves all made by craftsmen skilled in traditional techniques from the Veneto region.

Calle della Canonica | San Marco 318/A
micheledefina.it

Lellabella
SAN MARCO

In this tiny shop in a quiet corner of Venice. Mother and daughter owners, Lella and Monica, offer a broad array of fine yarns along with their own knitted creations and even knitting lessons, if you so desire. However, the old maxim of 'don't pull the wool over my eyes' may apply here as hidden behind the cupboard doors is a magnificent collection of luxuriant Italian scarves. Lellabella is one of my 'always-stops', a chance to drape myself in ultrafine pashmina, the softest cashmere, virgin wool and stunning prints, topping up on Italian style and take-home memories of Venice.

Calle della Mandola | San Marco 3718
labellavenezia.com

Fanny Gloves
SAN POLO AND CANNAREGIO

Leather gloves have long been a staple of
Venice, and Fanny's handsome range offers
the chance to treat yourself to a pair of
fur-lined kid gloves or a lambskin polka-dot
pair lined with cashmere.

Two Locations:
Calle dei Saoneri | Campo San Polo 2723
San Leonardo | Cannaregio 1647
fannygloves.it

Micromega
SAN MARCO

For eye-turning and feather-light handmade
spectacles and sunglasses, head to Micromega.
Their creations encapsulate the meaning of
luxe and brim with finesse. Clients can choose
from more classic styles through to the self-
proclaimed 'fancy range' where imagination
has taken full flight with glasses in the form
of leaves, flaming suns and even hands. All
models can be customised with buffalo horn
and titanium.

Calle delle Ostreghe | San Marco 2436
micromegaottica.com

SHOES

These shoe shops regularly find favour with the dogged art hounds proudly supporting Italian artisan traditions. In no particular order:

Baldinini
SAN MARCO

A sleek interior is the backdrop for Baldinini's smart and glamorous shoes with attitude and attention to distinctive detail.

Mercerie del Capitello | San Marco 4924
baldinini-shop.com

Fratelli Rossetti
SAN MARCO

When you next see a man, most probably Italian, wearing a tasselled loafer without socks, know that it was Fratelli Rossetti who were amongst the initiators of this trend back in the 1960s. The now-classic Brera loafer, complete with iconic tassel, made for both men and women, is stylishly updated each season in special colours and leathers.

Two locations:
Salizada San Moisé | San Marco 1477
Campo San Salvador | San Marco 4800
fratellirossetti.com

Pollini
SAN MARCO

From the renowned Italian maker Pollini, shoes with polish and poise that are also elegantly playful.

Sotoportego del Capello Nero | San Marco 186
pollini.com

Giovanna Zanella
CASTELLO

If you are seeking originality, then Giovanna Zanella's theatricality and use of exotic leathers (think toad or fish) should appeal. She possesses an innate understanding of form often sculpting her bespoke shoes from one piece of leather, but she is equally adept at using fabric and even plastic in her ready-to-wear designs. Zanella welcomes eccentricity from those who commission custom-made shoes encouraging them to even consider the possibilities of an asymmetric design. All hail to the passionate artisan with boundless imagination.

Calle Carminati | Castello 5641
giovannazanella.it

Beauty and Health

Antiques

Farmaceutica di Santa Maria Novella
SAN MARCO

Four hundred years in business and counting, they must be doing something right. This famed Florentine apothecary is renowned for its powders, soaps and fragrances, manufactured using a combination of traditional methods and newer innovations. Step into its suitably antiquated Venice branch and immerse yourself in a delirium of extracts, essences, perfumes and herbal remedies.

Salizada San Samuele | San Marco 3149
www.smnovella.it

Doriana Magnana
SAN MARCO

Trust an artist's eye and cast your gaze upon the window of jeweller and dealer in antique jewellery near Campo Santo Bartolomeo.

San Marco 5536

Abode

Mariano Fortuny Design
GUIDECCA

Heaven is just a boat ride away for lovers of
interior design and textiles, their destination
being the Fortuny Factory showroom on
Giudecca Island. Here, on weekdays, they can
linger lovingly, admiring Mariano Fortuny's
legacy of fabrics that speak of tradition but
in a modern voice, even 100 years later. The
fabrics are distinguished by their graphic
strength, fluid line and delicate dyes in refined
hues. Eighty per cent of the work is still done
by hand following the closely guarded secret
treatments of the master himself. Cushions,
bags and also lighting are available.

Giudecca 805
fortuny.com

Venetia Studium
SAN MARCO

Lino Lando established his studio in 1984 with
the aim of creating textiles that would revive
and build upon the art and design culture of
Venice. The company's design projects are
now all over the world, from the Criterion
restaurant, London, to the Four Seasons Resort,
Dubai. Curtains, cushions, fabrics as well as
clothing, bags and scarves are infused with the
East-meets-West spirit in jewel-toned velvets and
silks. Venetia Studium has the exclusive licence
to produce Fortuny Lamps, which can be bought
from their online shop. There are three stores
in Venice.

Flagship Store:
Calle delle Ostreghe | San Marco 2428
venetiastudium.com

Interior designer and creative director of Anna Spiro textiles, Anna Spiro, suggests a visit to the historic Fortuny fabric house:

'They produce some of the finest fabrics in the world. It's amazing and was created by artist Mariano Fortuny in 1907. You can go there and see where they design and print the fabrics.'

Dana Tomić Hughes of the ultimate design blog, *Yellowtrace* recommends stopping by the Japanese-influenced Olivetti Showroom, home of the Olivetti typewriters and calculators:

'Carlo Scarpa's Olivetti Showroom is a little gem and a true masterpiece. Even though it's located directly on the main Piazza San Marco, many people could miss it due to its inconspicuous street frontage.'

NasonMoretti
MURANO

Murano glassmaker, NasonMoretti, fires
the imagination with its objects, lights and
tableware in a handsome range of classic
designs. However, my heart lies firmly with
the modern range where it is almost impossible
to choose between 'Idra's' textural mash-up,
the super-fine filigree of 'Canova' or 'Dandy's'
dreamy melding of clear and opaque
liquefied colour.

Calle Dietro Gli Orti 12 | Murano
nasonmoretti.it

Caigo da Mar
SAN MARCO

A sensuous *wunderkammer* that lures you in with
luscious scents from the candles of Cire Trvdon,
established in 1643, and then delights with an
array of tempting *objets* for homes dedicated to
la bella vita, such as the oh-so-Italian Fornasetti
ware. Decorative peacocks and butterflies,
both vintage and modern, adorn the rooms of
Caigo da Mar and you may just find yourself
tucking a unicorn under your arm – yes, magic
does happen.

Calle delle Botteghe | San Marco 3131
caigodamar.com

Chiarastella Cattana
SAN MARCO

Chiarastella Cattana's fresh and smart jacquard
collection clearly aligns with the maxim 'less is
more'. Cattana's designs are inspired by flora,
fauna and the architectural language of Venice
infused with a contemporary edge whilst still
keeping an eye on the past. Let yourself be
tempted by her whisper-thin linen napkins,
handsome tablecloths, gorgeous bath linens,
modern classic cushions and exquisite bespoke
embroidered cotton sheet sets that take up to
half a year to be made.

Salizada San Samuele | San Marco 3216
chiarastellacattana.com

Mementoes

GLASS JEWELLERY & OBJETS D'ART

Marina and Susanna Sent
MURANO

These sisters, steeped in the traditions of
Murano, bend glass to their highly creative
and innately stylish will. Their jewellery
and *objets d'art* expose the special properties
of glass through a minimalist and elegant
structure expressed with fluidity and a
contemporary aesthetic.

Fondamenta Serenella 20
marinaesusannasent.com

LEATHER

Il Gufo Artigiano
SAN POLO

An artisanal treasure lies near the fish markets
of San Polo, which although tricky to find, is
worth the endeavour. Inside the intimate space
of 'The Artisanal Owl' vegetable-dyed animal
leathers are deftly crafted into hand-bound
sketchbooks, containers, wallets and handbags,
all embossed with Venetian designs or the
iconic Lion of St Mark, in a colour from the rich
Renaissance palette. These charming goods
embody the authentic hand and soul of Venice's
craftsmanship, in a rapidly disappearing space.

Ruga dei Spezieri | San Polo 299

MASKS

Ca'del Sol Venezia
CASTELLO

If you fancy a bit of mystery, role-playing or glamour, then look no further than the decadent and flamboyant mask creations of Ca'del Sol Venezia. By contrast, the Pierrot mask is eerie, inherently evocative, conveying the power that these superbly crafted and composed masks can possess. I gather that these masks are more likely to adorn the wall than aid disguise.

Campo San Zaccharia | Fondamenta Osmarin
Castello 4964
cadelsolmascherevenezia.com

PAPER

Gianni Basso Stampatore
CANNAREGIO

In a digital world Gianni Basso's profession as a letterpress printer has become a rarity, however his cards, bookplates and bespoke stationery are in high demand by those who appreciate time-honoured traditions. Basso was trained by Armenian monks in the ancient craft on pre-industrial presses and he has since become renowned for his refined workmanship. In keeping with the nature of his practice, Basso only accepts commissions in person or by post, putting a firm stamp on his terms of business.

Calle del Fumo | Cannaregio 5306

Fabricharte
CASTELLO

As the city of letters during the Renaissance, Venice was the epicentre for printing and publishing and Fabricharte continues the proud legacy producing custom-made books (including address and notebook options), employing traditional book-binding methods as well as creating photo albums, frames and fine patterned papers.

Barbaria dele Tole | Castello 6477/A
fabricharte.org

Relish

The Art Cognoscenti's Favourite Haunts

It's fair to say that while visitors to Venice may be enthralled by its sights, they are not always so taken by its tastes. Venice's restaurant reputations are undermined by pockmarked perceptions and often, visitors will search for typical 'trademarked' Italian classics such as *Spaghetti alla Carbonara* in a region where seafood-based fare abounds. I say, abandon these widely shared impressions, neutralise your expectations and start fashioning your own experiences away from the white noise.

When in Venice

The Venetian Lagoon has resoundingly shaped the history, the architecture and the palates of its citizens. Brimming with sea life, these waters have provided the Veneto with a rich harvest of clams, cuttlefish, squid, sardines, sole, oysters, eels and the like for centuries, forging a cuisine far removed from the earthy gastronomy of nearby Tuscany. The Venetians' recipes are marked by a lightness of touch, riffing off the freshness afforded by food caught just moments away from the plate. The influence of other cultures woven into Venice's embellished cloak are also manifest in recipes laden with spices from Byzantium, whilst the spring soup *Risi e bisi* (rice and peas) and seafood risotto owe their core ingredient to trade with the Arabic world.

In a region dominated by polenta and rice, the Venetians can still lay claim to one pasta incarnation of their own: *bigoli*. This thick and coarse wholewheat spaghetti is the perfect vessel for the Veneto's favoured sardine-based meal, *Bigoli in salsa*. Ironically, one marine-inspired dish, *Baccalà mantecato*, is not sourced from local shores but was introduced in the 15th century from Norway, a reminder of the cosmopolitan nature and reach of *La Serenissima*. It's arguably the most iconic local *cicheti*, or bar snack, but non-Lagoon dwellers may not have the same gastronomic enthusiasm for this creamed, dried salted cod atop bread or polenta.

Now with eyes wide open and a morsel of knowledge tucked in your back pocket, venture forth, armed with this list of local and on the quiet. eateries that have been scrutinised and hand selected by my generous and ever-discerning art confrères – tastemakers and cultivated denizens of the world. You are ready to navigate and savour the culinary maze of Venice – *mangia!*

Relaxed

Osteria Enoteca San Marco
SAN MARCO

One of my favourite dining haunts, just a few streets from Piazza San Marco, dispels any notions that you can't escape the tourist slant that casts a pall over this prime location. Once a tavern, its heritage is upheld through its fulsome and considered wine list. Service is crisp but attentive and the menu caters to carnivores, pescatarians and vegetarians in equal measure. Dishes focus on a handful of ingredients, which – in the best of Italian culinary tradition – allows the flavours to shine through. Make sure you try one of the seasonal pasta dishes like the black squid ink spaghetti or the delicious burnt butter ravioli.

Calle Frezzeria | San Marco 1610
osteriasanmarco.it

Rossopomodoro
SAN MARCO

When you find yourself near San Marco Piazza and have only 30 minutes to spare, escape here and try the 5 Formaggi pizza. Rossopomodoro boasts one of the city's few wood-fired ovens, which are limited due to safety restrictions (yes, romantic candle-lit hotel rooms are a no-no).

Calle Larga | San Marco 404
rossopomodoro.it

Hosteria Al Vecio Bragosso
CANNAREGIO

With seafood sourced from the nearby Rialto markets, Bragosso, a type of fisherman's boat, is an inexpensive restaurant with an authentic Venetian menu where fish is the hero.

Strada Nuovo | Cannaregio 4386
alveciobragosso.com

Aciugheta
CASTELLO

A smart modern trattoria, Aciugheta offers a quick fix of *cicheti* and local wine at the bar or casual dining where pizza takes the prize and pasta follows close on its heels. It very democratically shares a kitchen with its sister restaurant next door, the 1-star Michelin restaurant, Il Ridotto, which explains why the ingredients sing.

Campo SS. Filippo e Giacomo | Castello

Corte Sconta
CASTELLO

Quietly tucked away from the crowds but also conveniently close to the Arsenale for all the Biennale hounds. This is the perfect place to break and sit beneath the cooling vines in the courtyard or calm your mind by counting the colours within the terrazzo floor as you enjoy fabulous seafood prepared with love and finesse. At a pinch, the soft shell crab is one of the headline acts.

Calle del Pestrin | Castello 3886
cortescontavenezia.com

CoVino
CASTELLO

With only seven tables, this father and son-run establishment caters for just two sittings a night. My exquisitely attuned New York gallerist friend, Andrea Cashman advises that the special tasting menu is the go.

Calle del Pestrin | Castello 3829a
covinovenezia.com

Trattoria da Remigio
CASTELLO

A trusted eatery favoured by the city's inhabitants who countenance its classic Venetian fare. I am told by Simon Mordant, a former Venice Biennale Commissioner for Australia, and exceedingly well-travelled gentleman, that the seafood risotto is a must.

Salizada dei Greci | Castello 3416

La Zucca
SANTE CROCE

While not exclusively vegetarian, true to its name (*zucca* means pumpkin) this restaurant celebrates vegetables and is the cream of the crop for Australian artist, Shaun Gladwell. The seasonal menu respects Venetian traditions but imbues them with its own modern, informal touch. This osteria is tucked in a quiet *calle* alongside a canal in Santa Croce, but as there are only 40 seats it might be wise to make a reservation during the busy months.

Sotoportego del Tintor 1 | Santa Croce 1762
lazucca.it

'In Venice, one does not grab a sandwich for lunch on the hop or refuse a decent drop of wine. One sits and savours, drawing out the midday meal.'

Susan Kurosawa

Classic

Osteria Antica Adelaide
CANNAREGIO

Reviews and renews culinary classics and
serves them in the good company of all
manner of organic, biodynamic and
traditional wines in an atmospheric setting.

Calle Priuli Racheta| Cannaregio 3728

Ristorante Fiaschetteria Toscana
CANNAREGIO

Leave it to the sophisticated Italians to
understand the power and art of simplicity.
Here at Fiaschetteria Toscana the fish is king
and able to shine with the accompaniment of
just a few harmonious ingredients.

Salizada S.Giovanni Grisostomo
Cannaregio 5719
fiaschetteriatoscana.it

Stylish

Al Covo
CASTELLO

Dedicated to the slow food movement and driven by quality, Al Covo's stellar menu and wine cellar are studded with locally sourced and biodynamic produce. This restaurant's intimate scale certainly belies its ambition and success. Situated between the Arsenale and San Zaccaria it offers a perfect respite for the Biennale long-haul adventurers.

Calle della Pescaria | Castello 3968
ristorantealcovo.com

Riviera
DORSODURO

If you yearn to sit alongside the Adriatic but not be sustained entirely by its seafood bounty then Riviera may be the answer as pork, beef and veal as well as fine seafood are on the contemporary menu. Al fresco dining offers expansive views across to Giudecca Island with the option of choosing from a degustation, set or a la carte menu.

Zattere| Dorsoduro 1473
ristoranteriviera.it

L'Osteria di Santa Marina
CASTELLO

Refinement rather than radical reinvention is the name of the game in a restaurant much loved by wealthy Venetians. However, that's not to say that creativity does not come into play in the inventive presentation of the largely seafood-inspired dishes and the blend of classic and modern Mediterranean flavours. Sporting a wonderful wine list, this establishment is run with great passion and precision.

Campo Santa Marina | Castello 5911
osteriadisantamarina.com

Hotel Monaco & Grand Canal
SAN MARCO

A typically discreet entrance, just across from that other institution, Harry's Bar, adds to the frisson of exclusivity and unexpected seclusion of the celebrated Hotel Monaco. Head directly for the terrace with its crisp buttery yellow tablecloths and riotous red geraniums, your chichi sunglasses affixed with a jaunty attitude. Order a house specialty of *Tartare di Salmone e Pesce Spade al Limone e Basilico* and a refreshing Veneto *vino bianco* for lunch whilst drinking in the eye-catching Grand Canal views and the noble pastime of voyeurism.

Piazza San Marco | San Marco 1332
hotelmonaco.it

Beyond the Mediterranean

Il Ridotto
CASTELLO

This 1-star Michelin restaurant reinterprets classic regional traditions, imbuing fragrant notes of the Orient through subtle touches of lemongrass, bergamot and ginger. This contemporary philosophy also reverberates in the modish and elegantly laidback interior featuring exposed brick complemented by crisp white tablecloths and luxuriant leather and chrome chairs.

Campo SS. Filippo e Giacomo | Castello 4509
ilridotto.com

Basara Milano
SAN MARCO

Japanese cuisine meets Venetian style with this unexpected dining option. Like origami, Basara is multi-faceted: after the lunch service it transitions to a patisserie (pastries, coffee and aromatic teas) followed by happy hour, which brings a change in pace and space as sliding doors re-orient the restaurant in preparation for its evening sushi service.

Campo San Gallo | San Marco 1089
basaramilano.it

Delivery & Porta Via

Lino Fritto
SAN POLO

Lino Fritto offers an uncommon service in Venice – home delivery – and conveniently provides online ordering in English. It is seafood but not as you know it; salmon crumbed with sesame seeds and presented on an ice-cream stick is one of their specials. Situated near *La Pescaria* (the fish market) and Rialto Bridge, its artistic display may also tempt you with its *porta via* (take-away) options.

Mercato di Rialto | Campo de le Becarie 319
linofritto.it

GELATO

Gelatoteca SuSo – SAN MARCO
Voted best gelato in Venice
by *The New York Times*.

•

La Mela Verde – CASTELLO
My personal favourite and good
value gelato favoured by locals.

•

Gelateria Lo Squero – DORSODURO
Famous among the jet set – a
favourite of the Brad and Angelia
that was…and all the kids.

Carouse

Venice's Hidden Wine Bars

There are only two ways to slice it when it comes to imbibing during the aperitivo hour in Venice. You can opt for maximum glamour, taking in the most ravishing venues and views of Venice. Or, if you prefer a more earthly and understated adventure then wander and wassail between the local bacari, or bars, thereby honouring a pastime that the Venetians term *giro di ombre*.

Luxe bars at Venice's haute hotels

Here is a selection of fabulous, intimate and
often spellbinding sites to rendezvous...but be
warned – once you have sipped ambrosial nectar
from a crystal glass on a sultry Venetian evening,
you will forever be under the city's spell.

Bar Terrazza Danieli – Hotel Danieli
CASTELLO

Spritz...and a killer view. There is no better
place than this utterly glamorous venue to
gaze upon the Grand Canal, whilst catching
glimmers of the late afternoon sunlight across the
water. Not too shabby for a sunset Bellini either.

Riva degli Schiavoni | Castello 4196
danielihotelvenice.com

B Bar – Bauer Hotel
SAN MARCO

A luxurious clubby bar, all dark leather seats,
classic cocktails and moody lighting, and a hot
spot for celebrity and people-watching.

San Marco 1459
bauervenezia.co

GIRO DI OMBRE

*A Venetian term for bar-hopping, its
pure translation is 'turn of the shadow'.
Convention says that it originates from
the time when wine merchants plied
their trade in San Marco Piazza and
sheltered their barrels in the shadows
(ombre) of the bell tower. In modern
times,* ombra *refers to a small
measure or token of wine enjoyed at the
local* bacari, *alongside the bite-sized
savoury snacks called* cicheti.

Gabbiano Bar – Belmond Hotel Cipriani
GIUDECCA

Here you can sit poolside sipping on an
aromatic cocktail of elderflower liqueur,
passionfruit and prosecco – a George
Clooney tribute to his mother, Nina.

Riva degli Schiavoni | Giudecca 10
belmond.com/hotel-cipriani-venice

Oriental Bar – Hotel Metropole
CASTELLO

Trompe l'oeil paintings, flourishes of baroque
and candlelight are the background to the lavish
cocktail and martini menu at the Oriental Bar.
Try the pomegranate version of the Venetian
Spritz or one a dozen or so other choices.
And the views are stunning.

Riva degli Schiavoni | Castello 4149
hotelmetropole.com

LOCAL QUAFFS

Bellini

*The combination of sparkling Prosecco and
the juice from sun-ripened, white peaches was
introduced to the world by Harry's Bar. Make
your pilgrimage to this Venetian institution at
the Hotel Cipriani to pay homage to Giuseppe
Cipriani, the originator of this joyful drop.*

Bar Longhi – The Gritti Palace
SAN MARCO

An intimate venue with trademark Venetian elegance – Murano glass, paintings by 18th-century Venetian painter Pietro Longhi – and a formidable cocktail list. In the warmer months, head to the terrace on the Grand Canal.

Campo Santa Maria del Giglio | San Marco
thegrittipalace.com

PG'S Bar – Palazzina G
SAN MARCO

High-tech meets high glamour in PG's Bar which bears the eclectic style of French über-designer Philippe Starck. Mahogany, metres of glass, touches of surrealism and a fashionable crowd stake out the bar. The hotel entrance is discreetly hidden away.

Ramo Grassi | San Marco 3247
palazzinag.com

LOCAL QUAFFS

Spritz

Introduced by the Austrians but infused with Venetian style, this summery aperitivo mixes white wine, sparkling water and the radiant red hues of Italian bitters, either Aperol or Campari. A dash of ice, a slice of lemon or lime, and you are ready to toast Venice. Cin cin.

Or perhaps you prefer a White Spritz – an equally refreshing blend of Prosecco, soda and lime.

Bacari – with a splash of authenticity and a dash of history

Bacari are casual, low-key establishments where you can indulge in a quick drink, enjoy an *aperitivo* or satisfy your oenophilic curiosity sampling the array of wines whilst grazing on fine food morsels. Don't be misled by their often unstylish, démodé and rustic décor; instead look for a crowd, listen for Italian and eat with your eyes. It is worth mentioning that the traditional character of the bacaro continues to inform nearly all aspects of business, with most still adhering to a cash economy.

Cantina Do Mori
SAN POLO

I often stop by to refuel in between art treks and shopping adventures at Venice's oldest bacaro, a mere six centuries old. Unless you can spot a barrel, it's a stand-up affair beneath a sea of copper pots in this tight, darkened medieval-proportioned space. The *cicheti* will soon revive your spirits and quash thoughts directed at mere mortal matters such as sore feet. Try the *tramezzini*, small but plump sandwiches with fillings such as tuna and olive or their own special version of the *francobollo* (a 'postage-stamp' size sandwich), filled with crab, prawn and ham.

San Polo 429

Cantina Do Spade
SAN POLO

Do Spade is the same vintage as Do Mori but with seats (!). Come here if you want to accompany your wine with food from a menu peppered with Venetian classics such as *Seppie in nero con polenta* (Squid in black ink sauce with polenta) and *Folpetti alla Veneziana* (Venetian-style baby octopus). The fried zucchini flowers stuffed with cod are delicious too.

San Polo 859
cantinadospade.com

La Cantina
CANNAREGIO

Opposite Palazzo Mora, La Cantina is highly regarded for its raw fish, freshly shucked oysters and nearly three dozen wines by the glass. Artist Michael Cook warns not to be deterred by its appearance, as it is splendid for people-watching in the sun while drinking good wine and Prosecco.

Campo San Felice| Cannaregio 3689

Osteria Al Timon
CANNAREGIO

Some might call it stalking, I prefer to call it research, following in the footsteps of a young, hip local who led me to this delightful osteria set alongside the picturesque Ormesini canal. In the afternoon you can ponder all the big stuff whilst imbibing wine and nibbling *cicheti*, then in the evening rock it out with live music that sometimes plays on the boat moored next to the canal.

Fondamenta degli Ormesini | Cannaregio 2754
timonvenezia.com

Un Mondo DiVino
CANNAREGIO

It's 'a divine world' indeed when you can pop in and savour appetizing *cicheti* and wine from such a wide range at this cosy, timber-lined wine bar.

Salizada San Canciano | Cannaregio 5984
unmondodivinovenezia.com

Il Paradiso Perduto
CANNAREGIO

Paradise has been found at this rustic *bacari*-cum-*osteria*, a popular local haunt known for its market-fresh seafood (try the fried salt cod) and live jazz. They say 'heaven can wait' as evidenced by the queues, so it's worth making bookings for dinner.

Fondamenta della Misericordia
Cannaregio 2540

Osteria Al Portego
CASTELLO

A tiny hole-in-the-wall osteria that pulls a local crowd. Stand at the bar and munch on tasty *cicheti* and inexpensive wine, or try to nab one of the eight or so tables to sample traditional local fare, mainly starring seafood with dishes including *Tonno alla Livornese* and black cuttlefish and fresh daily pasta.

Calle Larga Malvasia | Castello 6014

Enoiteca Mascareta
CASTELLO

Typically crowded and friendly, well regarded for its seasonal *cicheti* and seafood but particularly for the exceptional list of Italian wines.

Calle Lunga Santa Maria Formosa
Castello 5183
ostemaurolorenzon.com

Al Chioschetto
DORSODURO

A modest kiosk with outdoor seating only, but who wouldn't love sitting outside when it's under a shaded table, with a front-row seat to the sunset view along Giudecca Canal. It regularly turns into a party.

Fondamenta Zattere Al Ponte Lungo | 1406A
Dorsoduro

Cantine del Vino già Schiavi
DORSODURO

At the foot of a bridge this compact but heavily stocked cellar door is also a wine bar, where you can join other clients standing, as Italians do, sampling a regional tipple and feasting on their creative crostini combinations.

Fondamenta Nani 992
cantinaschiavi.com

Osteria I Rusteghi
SAN MARCO

A grand passion for wine is more than evident here where an astounding 800-plus varieties from Italy and France are on offer. Sit in the calm of the courtyard with a hand-selected glass of vino or perhaps a champagne and a plate of prosciutto tenderly cured for 27 months, or a *paninetti* of pork with truffle sauce, during a temporal escape from the madding crowds of Rialto.

Campiello del Tentor | San Marco 5513
osteriairusteghi.com

Chat Qui Rit
SAN MARCO

Epicurean delights and a smart interior beckon through the large glass windows of Chat Qui Rit, one of Venice's few contemporary wine bars and bistros. It's as much an aesthetic experience as a gastronomic one with cured meats hanging elegantly, a vertical garden, providore shelves filled with olive oil and pasta, benches with overflowing bowls of cherry tomatoes and lemons and cake stands brimming with *biscotti*. Chat Qui Rit is a welcome retreat after the bustle of nearby Piazza San Marco where you can enjoy freshly prepared *antipasto* as the waiter pours you a wine, or you can stay for a meal. It also caters to vegans – happy days!

Calle Tron | San Marco 1131
chatquirit.it

Repose

Slumber in style

If you are contemplating whether to stay on Venice Island or on the mainland at Mestre, there is no question. To fully immerse yourself in the true Venetian experience, it's really more a matter as to which sestiere on the island you will choose to call home, and the type of abode you will choose to lay your head.

From Palazzo to Apartamento

Venice spoils us with choice from Renaissance palazzi converted to hotels of epic grandeur and magnificence, to those with classic charm and an increasing number that offer contemporary luxe. Or perhaps you prefer the new economy and adventure of Airbnb.

Apartments are a fabulous option for the independent spirit. Also, sharing a big apartment with friends leaves more to splash on water taxis, upping both convenience, and most importantly, the glamour quotient in one.

Astute actor Rachel Griffiths recommends taking a well-located apartment in a residential piazza, as 'nothing beats tapping into its genuine atmosphere and palpable rhythm'. She suggests Piazza San Anzello and, in the offseason, Piazza San Margherita as 'it's very young and Venetian'.

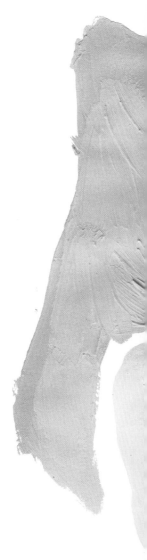

Susan Kurosawa, travel editor for *The Australian* sums up the Belmond Hotel Cipriani best.

'It's impossible not to fall in love with a hotel at which you arrive by motor launch and a waiter who looks like an Armani model presents you with a Bellini, made from fresh white peaches, and a thin slice of margherita pizza. Dine at Cip's Club on a canopied patio by the Giudecca Canal (try the baby shrimps from Lake Garda, simply dressed with olive oil and parsley) and keep an eye out for regular guest George Clooney sipping on head barman Walter Bolzonella's special cocktail, Goodnight Amigos, made with Casamigo tequila from Clooney and best mate Rande Gerber's Mexican distillery.'

True Venetian Class

Belmond Hotel Cipriani
GIUDECCA

Arriving on the hotel's private launch adds a
certain style, but everything at the 5-star Cipriani
on Isola della Giudecca is stylish. The hotel offers
exclusivity, relative seclusion, lovely gardens,
swimming pool, Michelin-starred restaurant,
romantic lagoon-side dining, spacious suites and
peerless views of Venice. At a price, of course.

belmond.com

Bauer Il Palazzo
SAN MARCO

Splendidly furnished and enjoying an enviable
position on the Grand Canal, Il Palazzo is
packed to the rafters with the art cognoscenti
during the Biennale. Loulou's, the pop-up
chapter of the London members-only club in
the hotel's sumptuous art deco BBar is the
hottest ticket for after-dark Biennale partying.

ilpalazzovenezia.com

Hotel Danieli
CASTELLO

The legendary Danieli, brilliantly located on
the Grand Canal, exudes patrician elegance. Its
1930s extension is a particular favourite of many
creative beings, including Rachel Griffiths. The
flamboyant lobby has provided a backdrop for
movies such as *The Tourist* with Johnny Depp
and the 1970s James Bond classic *Moonraker*.

danielihotelvenice.com

The Gritti Palace
SAN MARCO

Lording it over the Grand Canal, the Gritti is
iconic and quite OTT. Painstakingly restored
and refurbished, it offers a heady mix of
luxurious 18th-century style and luxe Moderne.
Its dress circle position on the Grand Canal
across from the Peggy Guggenheim Gallery
adds further cachet.

thegrittipalace.com

Hotel Metropole
CASTELLO

This hotel's richly storied past – it was a church
where Vivaldi taught music, and hotel guests
have included Sigmund Freud and Marcel
Proust – is superbly Venetian. Rooms are
exotically and sumptuously furnished, while
lighting is moody and atmospheric. The
hotel's 1-star Michelin restaurant, MET takes
classic Italian cuisine and imbues it with artful
touches. Don't miss the fabulous Oriental Bar.

www.hotelmetropole.com

Lay on the Gilt

Ca'Sagredo Hotel
CANNAREGIO

Perfect if you are looking to surround yourself in the opulent interiors of Venice past whilst watching Venice present from your hotel window overlooking the Grand Canal. The Heritage Suites boasting 17th- and 18th-century stucco wall and ceiling decorations, frescoes by Giambattista Tiepolo and beautiful terrazzo floors befitting its former occupant, Count Sagredo, are testament to his family's multi-generational art patronage. The other hotel rooms also offer an embarrassment of riches with brocade, patterned wallpaper, luxuriant drapes and damask.

casagredohotel.com

Modern Classic

Hotel Londra Palace
SAN MARCO

A symphony of cream and soft accents greet guests in the foyer at this elegant Relais & Châteaux hotel overlooking St Mark's Basin perched along the pivotal Golden Mile. Its 53 rooms are individually and tastefully furnished with Biedermeier furniture and beautiful textiles and the hotel maintains an intimate boutique feel. Sit out on the street-level terrace to watch the passing parade as you enjoy, perhaps, a yogurt and fruit breakfast whilst sipping on your cappuccino.

londrapalace.com

Designer digs

Palazzina G
SAN MARCO

Philippe Starck reinterpreted and uplifted this palazzo into a 21st-century groove at the same time delightfully flashing its historical features and cred. It elegantly pays homage to Venice's affinity with mirrors and turns the glamour up to ten.

palazzinag.com

The Charming House
DORSODURO & CASTELLO

Actually three houses – two boutique hotels in Dorsoduro and design suite apartments in Castello, all very roomy and distinguished by their luxe, streamlined style enhanced by a contemporary art collection. Well suited to the independent soul, but with breakfast offered each morning. The espresso coffee machine in each room is a welcome addition.

thecharminghouse.com

Aman Venice
SAN POLO

Impeccable historic credentials – a 16th-century palazzo in the Papadopoli family since the 1800s – and rooms that effortlessly blend designer luxury with original period features and exquisite furnishings. There are genuine Tiepolo frescoes and even that rare Venetian sight, a garden. More private house than hotel, with typically discreet Aman service.

aman.com

Casa Flora
SAN MARCO

A creative entrepreneurial partnership between the Romanelli hotelier family and six young international designers from the Design-Apart Project will result in luxury apartments catering to the design savvy traveller, who has so far not been well served in Venice. Elena Pardini of Casa Flora says: 'Guests will be able to go with our Venetian chef to Rialto Fish Market and learn how to select the best ingredients and how to cook them in the fully equipped house kitchen. This will be a sort of cooking class with the enrichment of Venice as scenario and food culture. We will also offer a service where one of the last custom shoemakers in Venice will come make you your own custom pair of shoes.'

casafloravenezia.com

Intimate

Novecento Boutique Hotel & Hotel Flora
SAN MARCO

Quirky, intimate and well-priced nine-room
hotel with attentive staff and a sweet courtyard
for breakfast. It is complemented by its more
traditional sister, the 40-room Hotel Flora;
a 17th-century palazzo, behind Calle XXII
Marzo, decorated with antiques and featuring
a beautiful, secret garden. A welcoming and
personal touch is a card at breakfast stating
'Handmade with Love' and the names of the
Romanelli family who have owned the hotel
for several generations.

novecento.biz

Palazzo Nani Bernardo
DORSODURO

For an authentic experience in a 16th-century
palazzo, you can stay in one of the two self-
catering apartments with a welcome by the
charming Countess Elisabetta Lucheschi, whose
family have owned the palazzo for centuries.
Set proudly on the Grand Canal, it hides a
special treasure: a wonderfully lush, large
garden – the perfect place for breakfast al fresco
or respite and a Spritz on a hot summer's day.

palazzonanibernardo.it

Casa de Uscoli
SAN MARCO

This hidden gem, located near the
Accademia, exudes personality and immense
style. The generously proportioned suites
with windows overlooking the Grand Canal
are individually and creatively decorated
with distinctive rugs, contemporary and
classic paintings and splashes of modern
design that project a playful, character-filled
quality. A true insider's haunt, generously
revealed by international art advisor,
Amanda Love.

secretplaces.com/hotels/italy/venice/
venice/casa-de-uscoli

Going it Alone

Venice Prestige
ALL AREAS

London-based company Venice Prestige offers a dazzling array of seriously smart and stellar apartments in three categories – Prestige, Designer and Classic – across all quarters of the city. You may want to try them all. Beware, perusing photos of the high-end, luscious apartments could tip you into palazzo porn territory.

veniceprestige.com

VOV Collection
ALL AREAS

Balancing the scales on the luxury private accommodation front and bringing an enviable insider's edge and credentials to this specialised field is the Views on Venice Collection. The principals have tapped into their privileged local connections in order to offer lavish stays in stunning palazzi and handsome apartments. And just in case you have a longing to lodge on your very own island, they can satisfy this too. The villa on Isola Santa Cristina, 30 minutes from Venice, is set amongst vineyards, an apricot orchard and fisheries and is replete with its own yoga studio.

vovcollection.com

Venice Essentials

Before ever setting foot in Venice, many of us have travelled there in our mind, our journey sparked to life through the marvellous words and images conjured by artists such as Lord Byron, Ezra Pound, Ernest Hemingway and Henry James.

Here are some of the books and films that my friends have nominated as redolent of *La Serenissima*, traversing the spectrum from radiant to clandestine, erudite to colloquial and everything in between.

By the book

Sophie Calle's first artist book in 1980, *Suite Vénitienne* is a confession of desire, documenting her search for an elusive man and a relationship in a city echoing with the same intangibility. Calle later returned to Venice in a more prominent guise, representing France at the 2007 Biennale.

Death in Venice (1912), the classic novel of unfulfilled, tenuous desire by Thomas Mann conjures the passions that Venice can awaken.

The Comfort of Strangers (1981) by Ian McEwan is the perfect introduction for those intrigued by malevolence's cool embrace and the darker shadows of life.

The City of Falling Angels (2005) by John Berendt. This contemporary portrait of Venice, through a somewhat darkened prism, swirls around Berendt's investigation into the catastrophic fire destruction of the Fenice Opera House, then leads him to myriad characters embroiled in scandal, tensions and challenges.

The Glassblower of Murano (2006) and *The Venetian Bargain* (2014) by Marina Fiorato. If you are in the mood for murder and mystery, then Fiorato's light historical fiction, set in the city where she studied and has familial ties, might just set the right tone.

A Venetian Affair: A True Tale of Forbidden Love in the 18th Century (2005) and *Lucia: A Venetian Life in the Age of Napoleon* (2008) by Andrea di Robilant. The author is inextricably linked to the city, being a descendant of Venetian aristocrats. He delves into the fascinating lives of his relatives, one of whom was Lord Byron's landlady at Palazzo Mocenigo, thereby revealing an authentic portrait of the city in an authoritative voice.

Venice (1960) and *Ciao Carpaccio* (2014) by Jan Morris. Considered a modern classic, *Venice* deeply immerses the reader across a thousand years of the city's cultural history whilst still retaining a semblance of the mid-century period in which the book was written. Morris, an officer in the British Army was staioned there at the end of 1945 and charged with running the motorboats requisitioned by the force. He vividly evokes Venice's essence with humor, poignancy and above all, spirit, much like the city itself. You may also be tempted to read *Ciao Carpaccio* published almost six decades later. This amuse-bouche guides us through the works of Vittore Carpaccio, an artist to whom the author in the subtitle admits an infatuation with and whose reputation Morris would like to elevate, taking a magnifying glass to the animals, figures and symbols that populate the artist's work to illuminate thought.

A Thousand Days in Venice (2002) by Marlena de Blasi. Set in the 1980s, this true romance recounts the tale of an American chef and food writer who falls in love with a Venetian, as well as with the city's food and its markets. The book is suitably peppered with recipes.

The Wings of The Dove (1902) by Henry James. A dramatic tale of the intertwined destinies of three young people linked by love, desire, greed, hope and betrayal set at the turn of the century in London and Venice.

For further literary inspiration:
fictionalcities.co.uk/venice

The moving image

Das Venedig Prinzip (The Venice Syndrome) (2012)
The threats and pressing challenges facing
Venice are laid bare in this frank documentary.

Don't Look Now (1973)
This thriller by Nicolas Roeg, based on a book
by Daphne du Maurier is equally unsettling
and intriguing.

Summertime (1955)
The tale of an independent woman on
her dream holiday to Venice who finds her
loneliness magnified. However, a romantic
liaison and ironically the city itself ultimately
transform her into a more assured being.

The Merchant of Venice (2004)
This interpretation of Shakespeare's classic
drama set in 16th-century Venice imparts a
sense of a history we can never truly experience.

Dangerous Beauty (1998)
A Renaissance courtesan who enjoys influence
and plaudits for her political manoeuvring finds
her circumstances dramatically altered when
accused of witchcraft.

Pane e Tulipani (Bread and Tulips) (2000)
A complex and charming story where conventions
are broken, unexpected love is found in different
corners of Venice, challenges abound…and you
will need to see the film to learn the rest. Certainly
love and Venice seem to be inextricably linked.

The Venice Book

What to Pack

Now that the mind is somewhat nourished, let's move to matters more corporeal. This snapshot of the seasons aims to equip you with the knowledge for your Venetian wardrobe and itinerary. However, do not accept this as gospel because with the advent of climate change we are all learning that historical precedents may no longer prevail. So temper expectations, embrace inconsistency and unreliability, add some fluidity... and check forecasts before you pack.

Winter

Mist imbues Venice with a singularly ethereal and romantic character. The fog and rain seamlessly transport you to the potent and tangible historical corridors of the city invoking its bewitching qualities.

What to Wear

Envisage the concept of a powder-dry cocoon. Fluff out your coat (the ubiquitous puffer variety, if you must), and have waterproof footwear at the ready. Gloves and umbrellas are essential – have no fear, a plethora of glove shops are at hand.

Spring

Winter's firm grip is assuaged, making way for gentle showers and the soft and delicate warming rays of the sun. Muted tonal vistas transform to scenes of punctuated colour from the blooming wisteria, lilacs, tulips and violets; fragrant magnolia delights as spring beguiles with her graceful and intoxicating dance.

What to Wear

Conjure adaptability, airy lightness, refreshing breezes. Layering is the key and 'trans-seasonal' is the catch cry of the sartorially experienced and savvy.

VENICE KNOW HOW

Did you know that irons are not provided by hotels or short-term accommodation due to fire regulations? For the sartorially self-reliant pack a portable iron or, like me, a portable steamer... otherwise wear those creases with attitude.

•

If they could bottle 'effortless style' it would be called *uomo* for no one carries off the pastel linen jacket, crisp shirt, rolled up trouser and sockless shoe combo more tastefully and assuredly than the Italian man. I am yet to see a non-Italian pull off this ensemble with equal aplomb!

Summer

The island is noticeably pacier and bursting, in fact overflowing with energy. However, this is clearly powered by external elements and the dynamic and the tone is in a different key at this time of year.

Naturally the entrancing physical attributes of Venice remain unchanged, but with the onslaught of admirers and the evacuation of locals, the underlying, multi-faceted character of Venice retreats somewhat from view, along with some of its subtle and intriguing undercurrents. For high-season relief from the hordes, lasso the lull of early morn and early evening for your activities.

What to Wear

Breathe…Both as you move through the bustling streets of Venice and dressed in light cotton and stylish pre-crumpled linen clothing, with feet shod in stylish sandals and leather thongs – no rubber, please. A fan may prove to be especially useful for ameliorating the sticky and static air inside Venetian buildings.

Autumn

Civilised and restorative. Think blue-sky days and sunset amber-lit skies, geraniums bedecking balconies and ambrosial wafts of the often spice-laden hot chocolate that bears testament to Venice's Levantine heritage.

What to Wear

Trans-seasonal once more. Cooling days warmed by autumn sunshine that gives way to sudden heavy bursts of rain will be well met with a dashing raincoat and ankle boots. Light cashmere knits and featherweight silk and virgin wool scarves easily regulate your body temperature as you navigate the city in your mules, courts or designer sneakers.

Acknowledgements

Thank you to my sage, incisive and incredibly
supportive crew of advisers and enablers!

Kirsten Abbott

Tahlia Anderson

Margaret Barca

Del Kathryn Barton

Hans Berg

Giovanna Bertoni

Maike Brueggen

Andrea Cashman

Liza Chancellor

Sam Chatterton Dickson

Matteo Cozza

Andrew Cook

Michael Cook

Abigail Cox

Jane Devery

Nathalie Djurberg

Tony Ellwood

Shaun Gladwell

Dana Tomić Hughes

Simeon Kronenberg

Marita Lillie

Amanda Love

Rachel Griffiths

Eliza Mantello

Jan Minchin

Simon Mordant

Adam Obradovic

Elena Pardini

Lisa Paulsen

Georges Petitjean

Patricia Piccinini

Rosslynd Piggott

Olivia Poloni

Fiona Richardson

Sally Smart

Anna Spiro

Nicola Stein

Kandi and Ian Straker

Ursula Sullivan

Andy Taylor

Aida Tomescu

Daisy Tyszkiewicz

Albert Ullin

Claude Ullin

Margaret Ullin

Terry Wu

For Roland, Marco and Camilla Kautzky

Picture Credits

iii: Liza Chancellor; iv–v: Liza Chancellor; vi: (from top left) Mauro Grigollo/Stocksy United, Sophie Ullin, Danil Nevsky/Stocksy United; vii: (from left) Luca Pierro/Stocksy United, Liza Chancellor; viii: Liza Chancellor; 3: Nathalie Djurberg; 4: Liza Chancellor; 7: Liza Chancellor; 8: Danil Nevsky/Stocksy United; 9: Paulina de Laveaux; 10: Good Vibrations Images/Stocksy United; 13: (foreground) Marko Milanovic /Stocksy United, (background) solar lady/Stutterstock.com; 14: Liza Chancellor; 16: (foreground) Good Vibrations Images/Stocksy United, (background) Rodina Olena/Shutterstock.com; 18: Danil Nevsky/Stocksy United; 20: (foreground) Marko Milanovic/Stocksy United, (background) Tetiana Denysenko/Shutterstock. com; 22: Danil Nevsky/Stocksy United; 24–5: iStock.com/Roberto A Sanchez 33: (foreground) iStock.com/AndreyKrav, (background) solar lady/Shutterstock.com; 41: Gabriel (Gabi) Bucataru/Stocksy United; 42: Liza Chancellor; 47: tang/Shutterstock. com; 50–1: Liza Chancellor; 57: Sophie Ullin; 58: Sophie Ullin; 60: (foreground) Liza Chancellor, (background) Tetiana Denysenko/Shutterstock.com; 64–5: Juri Pozzi/Stocksy United; 67: Sophie Ullin; 72: photo.ua/Shutterstock.com; 74: Nathalie Djunberg; 77: Sophie Ullin; 80: courtesy of Patricia Piccinini; 87: (foreground) Sophie Ullin, (background) solar lady/Shutterstock.com; 98: (foreground) Fiona Richardson, (background) Rodina Olena/Shutterstock.com; 100: Jen Grantham/Stocksy United; 102: Kirstin McKee/Stocksy United; 105: iStock.com/walencienne; 107: courtesy of Transit Farm; 108: (foreground) Michela Ravasio/Stocksy United, (background) Tetiana Denysenko/Shutterstock.com; 109: Leander Nardin/Stocksy United; 110: Adam Obradovic; 111: Adam Obradovic; 113: Sophie Ullin; 116: Ron Mellott/Stocksy United; 123: (foreground) Julien L. Balmer/Stocksy United, (background) solar lady/Shutterstock.com; 124: Giorgio Magini/Stocksy United; 132: Lyuba Burakova/Stocksy United; 135: Liza Chancellor; 139: Oscity/Shutterstock. com; 142: Maja Topcagic/Stocksy United; 144: Jen Grantham/Stocksy United; 148: (foreground) Lyuba Burakova/Stocksy United, (background) Rodina Olena/Shutterstock.com; 154–55: Liza Chancellor; 156: Bratislav Nadezdic/Stocksy United; 158: Trent Lanz/Stocksy United; 164: Mauro Grigollo/Stocksy United; 165: Nicolas Cazard/Stocksy United; 170–71: Trent Lanz/Stocksy United; 172: Paulina de Laveaux; 177: Liza Chancellor; 181: Rebecca Spencer

First published in Australia in 2017
by Thames & Hudson Australia Pty Ltd
11 Central Boulevard Portside Business Park
Port Melbourne Victoria 3207
ABN: 72 004 751 964

www.thameshudson.com.au

ISBN: 978 050050 097 2

National Library of Australia Cataloguing-in-Publication entry

Creator: Ullin, Sophie, 1970- author
Title: The Venice Book / Sophie Ullin
ISBN: 9780500500972 (hardback)
Subjects: Art and architecture--Italy--Venice.
Tourism and art--Italy--Venice.
Venice (Italy)--Description and travel.

Design: Ortolan
Editing: Margaret Barca
Printed and bound in China by Imago